For T.
&
Cindy,

Warm aloha,

Faith

Home at Last

The True Story of a Desperate Pilgrim

FAITH COLLIER

Cover photo was taken by Susan Whitham from Duncan, B.C., Canada.
Cover design was created by Mike McDonald from Cleveland, Tennesse.
Cardinal sketches by Eileen Garrett from Cleveland, Tennessee.

Address all personal correspondence to:
Faith Collier
P.O. #223252
Princeville, HI 96722
justiceandfaith@holyliving.net

Individuals and church groups may order books from the author directly, or from the publisher. Retailers and wholesalers should order from our distributors. Refer to the Deeper Revelation Books website for distribution information, as well as an online catalog of all our books.

Published by:
Deeper Revelation Books
Revealing *"the deep things of God"* (1 Cor. 2:10)
P.O. Box 4260
Cleveland, TN 37320
423-478-2843
Website: www.deeperrevelationbooks.org
Email: info@deeperrevelationbooks.org

Deeper Revelation Books assists Christian authors in publishing and distributing their books. Final responsibility for design, content, veracity and factuality of stories and statements, permissions, editorial accuracy, and doctrinal views, either expressed or implied, belongs to the author. In most cases, the names of individuals in this book have been changed to protect their identity.

Dedication

*I dedicate this book to you, Justice, my husband and
fellow sojourner. You supported me in every way as I wrote, and
equally when I took long breaks and didn't write. No matter
where I was in the process of bringing forth this book, you were by
my side, providing me with the perfect encouragement. Thank you.
I also dedicate this book to all the desperate pilgrims who are deeply
seeking eternal love, joy and peace.*

Table of Contents

Acknowledgements

I am very blessed to have high-minded, articulate friends who were willing to read the first draft of this book and give me honest feedback.

Among those who spent a great deal of time taking in what I wrote, digesting it, and offering extremely valuable suggestions on how I could improve the manuscript were Warren and Joy Smith, Bob Hallman, Cindy Peterson, Lisa Barstow, Victoria Hamilton, Georgia Henderson, Richard Diamond, and Carol D. Anderson.

The final editing has been done by Mike Shreve, someone I consider to be a master linguist and a deep lover of God. How this great fortune came about, having a man of Mike's caliber personally care for the refinement and production of my book, can only be explained as pure grace. It is clear that the Lord is smiling on this project. I am very, very grateful.

Living on the island of Kauai on a magnificent waterway estate property has been the perfect retreat setting for me to write this book. It is by the kindness and ongoing generosity of Bill and Joan Porter that Justice and I have been given stewardship of this amazing Sanctuary. May many more books be written here, and countless lives benefited as a result of the philanthropic hearts of the Porters. When God calls, He provides.

Foreword

I found *Home At Last* to be a marvelous testimony of God's amazing grace, and of His patient and persistent pursuit of those souls who are truly seeking relationship with Him. Faith Collier has been on a long and winding road in her journey towards a truth-filled relationship with her Creator, Sustainer, Savior, and Lord. Faith has traveled deep into many of the popular spiritual disciplines under the far-reaching umbrella of the New Age movement, all of which left her unfulfilled, disappointed, sometimes devastated, and searching for true connection with God.

I first met Faith and her husband Justice when they began attending the church where I had been serving for several years. What I noticed was her incredible hunger for truth. I've had the privilege of watching Faith's appetite become satisfied as she immersed herself in the teachings of the Bible. Psalm 34:8 says *"Oh taste and see that the LORD is good; blessed is the man who trusts in Him!"* This book will give you a taste of the massive and miraculous capacity of God to redeem the mistakes, missteps, misfortunes and misgivings that often keep us distant from Him, and will invite you to enjoy the blessings of trusting Him.

Home At Last presents "snapshots" from various steps in Faith's journey that will grab your attention and keep you curious as to where this adventure leads. There's a saying that "all paths lead to God," but Faith's journey reveals that religious pluralism results in multiple dead ends. Jesus of Nazareth said of Himself, "*I am the way, the truth, and the life. No one comes to the Father except by me*" (John 14:6). Faith Collier discovered the way, truth, and life of Jesus Christ to be the "spiritual home" she had longed for all her life.

Home At Last is a refreshing look at how God can bring beauty from ashes, turn mourning into dancing, and put a new song in your heart. I pray that this book will find its way into the hands and hearts of other seekers and sojourners, so that its message might spare them from the detours and distractions in their own journey for truth.

Pastor Bruce Baumgartner
Calvary Chapel Lihue

Introduction

Someone who knows the authentic and valuable like the back of her hand will never be fooled.

Anne Nester loved to recite those words as she trained me to examine bills for their authenticity. I was not taught to discern the difference between the federal currency and the counterfeit by studying the cheap replicates along with the real thing. My boss told me that if I was intimately familiar with the genuine, I need not concern myself very much with the imitations. They would readily expose themselves. The counterfeit bills always looked different, felt different, and almost proudly proclaimed themselves to be different than the true bills.

Unfortunately, I wasn't working long enough under Anne Nester's supervision to get this important principle of money *and life* firmly under my belt. Before my first month at the Bank of America was over, I was fired.

Typically, when my boss wanted to speak with me she came directly to my work station, so she could see me in action. But this time was different. I was summoned to her office.

As I stepped beyond the threshold into Anne Nester's inner sanctum, I felt very uneasy. Something was brewing.

"You wanted to see me, Anne?" I ventured. My boss's eyes narrowed as she took in my faded jean mini-skirt and cowboy boots. Clearing her voice, Anne frantically corrected my casual

address one last time: "Mrs. Nester! Stop calling me Anne!!
Do you understand?! I'm Mrs. Nester!!"

I was definitely in trouble. Without a word, the contract
papers I had signed several weeks earlier were presented for my
inspection. Our agreements were clearly written in black and
white. I had actually promised to wear skirts below my knees
and conservative business shoes to work. There were policies,
protocols, standards, and order at this highly respected and
firmly established corporation, and I had not been compliant.
In fact, I had been defiant.

One thing I knew for sure; it was far too late for me to try
to defend myself. As my boss and I exchanged one final look of
total disbelief at one another, each of us clearly astonished that
she had hired me in the first place, I was shown the door.

That door led me out onto a wide, meandering, and very
rocky road of relentless pursuit.

The fundamental principles of the path I found myself on
were quite the opposite of what Anne Nester had been trying
to instill in me. The Nester approach was what is known in
India as *shastra* (shahstra); learning wisely from sanctioned authorities. The Goldstein (my name at the time) approach was
shastra (shustra); learning foolishly from the rod of correction.
At first glance, the two opposing ways, *shastra* and *shastra*, are
spelled identically and appear to be one and the same. But in
actuality, they are pronounced differently and are worlds apart.

The good news is that the spiritual path I chose did eventually lead me to the peace and fulfillment that I was desperately seeking. The bad news is that I suffered great anguish of soul
in the process. I was a lost and lonely pilgrim for a very long
time.

My hope and prayer is that you will learn to follow the

2

voice of the Master sooner rather than later. There really is no need or sound reason to learn from the painful correcting rod.

Lesson of the Cardinal

A beautiful red cardinal flew into my all-glass greenhouse kitchen through the open door one day while I was preparing lunch. As the bird viewed the mountains, trees, and sky through the glass walls, it naturally tried to return to the great outdoors by flying straight towards the wonderful scenery. The cardinal just could not comprehend that there was an impenetrable, invisible barrier preventing it from reaching its desired destination. Thus, it repeatedly bashed itself against the transparent walls, duped and misguided by the *illusion of freedom*.

I reached out in an attempt to direct the confused, enervated bird toward the only way to true freedom, the open door, but in its fearful, desperate state, the cardinal saw my extended hand as a threat. Rather than receiving my help, the poor bird thrust itself even harder and faster at the clear greenhouse walls. Finally, it came to the end of itself and fell to the floor, completely spent and broken. At this point, I was able to pick up the beautiful red cardinal, carry it outside through the open door, and gently place it on a tree. Several hours later, the bird received a second wind, and was restored to a state of wellbeing. The cardinal then flew off gracefully into the vast blue sky.

One More Chance

The utter heartbreak and anguish of my soul that I experienced in 1989 is not a condition that I can even begin to capture with words. I did not know that it was possible for a human being to go through such complete darkness and despair, and remain alive. My ability to function in the world was gone. Most of my time was spent crying my heart out on the floor of the completely bare apartment where I lived alone. Lifting my swollen eyes up high enough to count the tufts of gold colored carpet was about all I could summon up the will to do, as I railed against God for months on end. A final tirade brought closure to this abysmal lifestyle:

Where are you, God?! I have sacrificed for You and served You with everything I had to give. And, this is how You treat me? I'm at the end of my rope. I'm done. I can't go on. What kind of God are You, anyway? If You don't start reciprocating and put an end to this absolute torment that I'm in, well … forget it!

The following day after hurling this invective into the ethers of my empty living room, I heard a knock at the front door. My mother's frantic voice was screaming to me to let her in. How she knew that I was on the verge of suicide, I never found out. Somehow, my mother navigated her way from her waterfront home in Florida to my obscure little place in the hills of Alpine, California, just in the nick of time. She did not come alone. Sadie, a police woman, accompanied her.

Mom and Sadie kept vigil over me as I returned to the waterless bathtub where I had been lying corpse-like, grasping my vial of sleeping pills. After what seemed like hours of listening to the uniformed stranger talk, and hearing my mother's hysterical sobs, I felt something change inside of me. I was willing to give life *and* God one more chance.

A Drop of Hope

At the onset of my spiritual and emotional collapse, a friend of mine had offered to take my two young sons into her home, since I was incapable of caring for myself, let alone my children. Folding their clothes carefully and placing them in a suitcase, I said one last tearful goodbye to Matt and Drew in my heart. I wanted to appear stronger to my boys than I actually was when I gave them my parting hugs.

I had no idea how the situation would evolve. All I knew for sure was that it couldn't get any worse. With just a tiny bit of readiness and a mere speck of willingness, I was as ready as possible to step out and start a new life.

Because I couldn't even make it through a grocery check-out line or a gas station fill-up without going into a major panic attack, I supported myself with welfare checks from the government for almost a year. Anti-depressants from the doctors kept me from falling off the edge mentally.. Whenever I did venture out into the world, I became overwhelmed and paralyzed by the horrendous human predicament.

Don't these people know this world is meaningless? Why are they rushing around trying to find happiness and fulfillment in a world of false promises? Am I the only one here who feels like an alien and a stranger? Did I show up on the wrong planet, with the wrong God?

The "walking dead" existence that I endured during that time period was relatively unmemorable, except for one day when I followed my friend's seven-year-old daughter around for several hours. Chrissy escorted me to a beautiful lake and took me swimming. As I fell in step behind her, walking in her spritely footsteps and watching her strawberry blonde curls bounce around playfully, I felt just a drop of hope.

Something inside me relaxed. Maybe there would eventually be someone truly qualified who could lead me on the path of truth. Maybe—it would certainly take a miracle—but just maybe, I would be able to trust once again.

Spiritual Boot Camp

I had walked very closely in the footsteps of a renowned spiritual leader for twenty years before my life took the almost fatal nose dive I just described. He was known by his disciples as *jagad guru*, or the guru of the entire universe. Swami Prabhupada, an elderly Indian gentleman, had established 108 Hindu monasteries (*ashrams*) world-wide with some 15,000 followers. I became an initiated disciple of the well-known guru, and a radically-sold-out-devotee of that ancient religion.

The ashram studies, practices, and disciplines were all-consuming for me. As a result, I was fairly well equipped to be a spokesperson for the Hare Krishna Movement, as it was commonly known, on prime time national TV on several occasions, and in *Life* Magazine. Being interviewed by the talk show maestros of the day was a special treat for me. I fully enjoyed representing my guru and his mission to the multitudes.

The strict monastic life that we followed in the ashram suited my type-A personality very well. As difficult as it was to rise at 3 a.m. each day, sleep on the hard floor, take cold showers, practice strict celibacy, and immerse myself in Vedic studies, hours of chanting meditation, and tireless service, I loved the fact that every one of my thoughts, words, and actions was regulated with clear intention and purpose. The concepts of "casual" and "frivolous" did not exist in the ashram experience, which was just fine with me.

Despite the personal hardships I endured on the physical

plane, I was buoyed up on a spiritual plane by strong devotion to my guru. Swami Prabhupada was, according to my understanding at that time, the savior who would deliver me into the eternal kingdom of God. So, I held nothing back in my service and surrender.

Spiritual boot camp, as the ashram lifestyle was called, was an amazing training ground for my life, in a general sense. The predominating principle was absolute submission to higher authority, as one might encounter in the military or in prison. In fact, the disciples were referred to as "inmates" in the house of the guru. Once we entered the ashram and took our life-long vows, all of our personal rights were abdicated. It was not at all a problem for me to lay down those rights because frankly, I was materially exhausted—sick of what I considered to be a vain and empty existence—and I really didn't want to direct my own life anymore.

Being told how to breathe, eat, sleep, think, speak, sit, walk, dress, interact with people, make love, and every other intimate detail of daily life was actually a huge relief. It became easy to follow the ashram rules and protocols since any murmuring or complaining was generally met with a sarcastically dry admonishment, "It's Krishna's mercy, *prabhu* (master)!" So there really was no point in entertaining any discontent.

The holy laws or "regulative principles of freedom" as they were called, kept me focused and productive. The only thing that was conspicuously absent from my disciplined and set-apart life was love. Over the twenty-year time frame that I was immersed in that religion and culture, it was the lack of love in my heart that eventually wore me down to nothing—to the point where I could no longer function, and simply wanted to take my own life.

Solo Journey

In the condition I was in, emotionally destitute and spiritually bankrupt, there was not much I could do but desperately try to make sense out of my life. I was plagued with unanswered questions: *Why on earth did I ever move into a Hindu ashram in the first place to become a monastic nun? Why hadn't I been satisfied to just keep my job as a high school English teacher in San Francisco? And, what about my upbringing? Were all the upper middle-class Jewish values that I was raised with from birth no longer a part of who I was? Why?? Why?? Why??? My brother and sister were "normal." What happened to me? Was I the black sheep in my family, or did I just randomly turn out to be a wild card, relentlessly seeking after the ineffable?*

When I finally pulled myself together, enough to return to work full-time, I decided it would be worth the money to sort through my unresolved problems with a talk therapist. The weekly therapy sessions became a dependable life-line for me during that time of craziness and confusion. However,, I never could get to the root cause of my deep, soul-wrenching unhappiness.

In our last session together, my therapist, Richard, laid it on the line in a pointed and unforgettable manner. His final, very blunt and less-than-elegant words shook me to the center of my being: "There is no man out there who is going to save your *behind* (my paraphrase)!" Well, that's what it all came down to, didn't it? I was looking for a man to save me from the

12

emptiness and disappointments of temporal life in this material world.

I had recently given up on the idea that the guru was my savior who would deliver me into an eternal life of bliss in the spiritual realm. Then, lo and behold, I was told to forget about any man ever being my knight in shining armor who would whisk me away to some Never-Never Land (or should I say, Ever-Ever Land?). I knew Richard was right. No matter how wonderful intimate relationships might be, ultimately, I was on a solo journey. No guru had the power to give me the sense of home that my soul deeply longed for, nor did any ordinary man. I concluded that I was going to have to get busy and just create my own pathway back to the everlasting kingdom.

My True Identity

The pathway I chose to explore was to go within. I had often heard it said that "if you don't go within, you will end up going without." Since I was already *without* almost everything I truly wanted, I concluded that deep introspection would probably be the surest route to radical positive change.

I began by examining my childhood and paying special attention to unforgettable incidents and conspicuous patterns. What kept jumping out at me was a remarkable, unquenchable yearning for my true spiritual identity. As I grew up, this desire was interwoven throughout the entire tapestry of my life: every choice, every change and every major event.

My earliest memories were of age six. By that time, I already started resenting being born into a Jewish family. My parents told me it was a blessing to be from the Jewish blood line, that I was one of God's chosen people, but I just wasn't satisfied. In fact, for some odd reason, I thought I wanted to be a Christian.

It wasn't so much the issue of not being able to celebrate Christmas that made me look to Christianity as a more desirable belief system, (though that was a contributing factor). Mainly, there was something profoundly mysterious about Jesus Christ and His followers that drew me, setting me on a quest for a more complete understanding of God than what was passed down to me through Judaism. I couldn't really tell anyone about this spiritual longing because I was such a young girl, but I was painfully divided in my innermost parts.

I can look back now and identify certain dramatic events that God used to call me beyond the Jewish beliefs and traditions of my family. It all started with one soul-stirring episode when I was alone in the kitchen one day with my orthodox Jewish grandmother, *bubbie* (Yiddish word for grandma). Bubbie and I were preparing a snack when I decided to ask her who Jesus Christ was. I was simply curious. To me, my question felt harmless and innocent, but apparently, not to her. I was shocked at what happened.

Bubbie went ballistic, screaming at the top of her lungs, "Don't you *ever* mention that NAME in this house, *ever* again!!" Terrified, but still compelled to continue, I managed to summon up enough courage to ask one more question. "Why not?" I squeaked out, almost inaudibly. "Because you are Jewish!" she yelled, glaring at me with a look of 100% finality. I suppose my bubbie figured it was in my DNA to understand, because she gave no further explanation.

The reality was that I didn't understand, and my curiosity only grew stronger. *Who was Jesus Christ anyway? Why did the mere mention of His name send my grandmother through the roof?* I determined to find out. Somehow I sensed that if I had inquired about just about any other famous personality—a politician, a movie star, a professional athlete—there would have been no emotional outburst, but rather a simple, direct answer. Jesus must really be special and important if I'm not even allowed to find out anything about Him!

I began to take note of the Christian kids in my elementary school to see if there was anything different about them. As far as I could tell, some of them wore crosses and went to church on Sundays, but for the most part, they were just ordinary kids.

15

They played the same games that I did, watched the same TV programs, and fought with their siblings, just as I did. But it was the church-going and the whole mystique around Jesus that captured my mind. I decided to invite one Christian girl home for lunch and get to know her outside the school environment.

My mother had pretty much of an open-door policy at our home. Neighborhood kids would come in and out of our house without needing to be announced, so I didn't foresee a problem asking Sue over. But, when I mentioned to my mom that I wanted to have a classmate come for lunch the next day, she looked at me sideways and asked accusingly, "Is she Jewish?" Without leaving any time or space for me to answer, my mother emphasized her point. "A *shiksa* (a gentile girl)? What's the matter, you don't have enough Jewish friends?"

My little child's heart became heavy. I couldn't understand why my mother and her mother both had one-track minds. Didn't they care if someone was nice, or fun, or good at school? Why was the big issue whether or not they were Jewish? I realized that it wasn't going to work for me to befriend any *goyum* (gentiles) by bringing them home to meet my family.

I also became somewhat cautious about interacting with Christian children at school. There definitely seemed to be some kind of inborn dynamic in my lineage similar to the Montague/Capulet family feud that Romeo and Juliet had to contend with. But, when I faced my true feelings deep down inside, I recognized that I had the heart and spirit of a Juliet. Immature as I was, I knew that there was no one and nothing that could stop me from living my own life and coming to my own conclusions. I wasn't buying into something, just because it had been passed down for many generations.

For the next few years, I kept my eyes on my Christian classmates, wondering if I would ever get to attend a real church service. My parents took me to synagogue a few times a year on High Holy Days, and I always enjoyed the services, even though they were mostly in Hebrew. Still, while I was listening to the rabbi and cantor, my mind would wander, trying to imagine what it would be like to be worshiping in a church.

Why do the Christians get to go to church once or twice a week, and we only come to the synagogue three or four times a year? Does God love the Christians more than He loves the Jews? I thought we were the chosen ones? Chosen for what—suffering and exclusion?

The feeling of being deprived and second-class was a strong reality in me, especially when I was inside the Jewish temple and not really experiencing anything that I could wrap my mind around. It seemed more about the new clothes everyone was wearing and the families being together than about having a supernatural encounter with a living God. There was definitely something missing for me.

In my heart, I sensed that Christians had what I really wanted, but I didn't even know exactly what that was. There seemed to be a special, private club that followers of Christ had been born into that was absolutely exclusive. There was no opening for Jews, whatsoever, as far as I could tell. I was afraid that it was my destiny to always be on the outside of this club, jealously trying to figure out what was going on inside.

Finally one day, a very popular girl in my school, Laura Marten, invited me to her home. I was super excited. Not only was she beautiful, talented, loved by the student body, smart, and friendly—she was a Christian! Of course, when I proposed the visit to my mother, I got the standard response,

"Is she Jewish?" "No, Mom" I said, bursting into tears. I definitely had it with the Jewish thing. This was too much. I can't remember what happened, but my mother ended up relenting and allowing me to go to Laura's house.

Entering Laura's home was spellbinding for me. I looked around every corner as if I expected Jesus Christ Himself to step forward! Of course, I knew the Martens were regular people, with regular jobs, regular furniture, etc., but still, there was a different quality, an uplifting peace that seemed to permeate their living quarters. Then I saw what it was that was different. On the night stand next to Laura's parents' bed was a thick black leather book with gilded edges. I glanced surreptitiously at the title of the book: The Holy Bible. Wow! What a title! I certainly had heard about the Bible, but The *Holy* Bible. Now, that was something to behold.

This amazing book was like none other I had ever seen. Sure, it was just a book—a binding with printed pages—but I found myself irresistibly drawn to it, as if it were the forbidden fruit. I knew eventually I would open one of those very special Bibles and read it with all of my heart. What I didn't know was that such a life-changing event wouldn't take place for decades to come.

I wanted to ask some questions about Christianity, but I didn't know where to start, so I simply asked Laura why Christians liked crosses so much. I liked them too, but I had no idea what they represented. "Jesus was nailed to the cross," Laura answered very matter-of-factly, taking for granted that I had some background on the crucifixion. *Huh? Jesus nailed to a cross?* She continued to explain, as my young mind tried to sort through the details. Finally, Laura declared quite nonchalantly that the Jews killed Jesus, probably not realizing that my Jewish

18

roots were being jolted. I was absolutely shocked.

Could this be true? The Jews killed Jesus? I was starting to get a clue as to why my family wasn't particularly eager to mingle with Christians, and why there were Yiddish neighborhoods and Goyish neighborhoods. Feeling sick at heart, I just kept my mouth shut after that and realized that there was a lot I didn't know, and wasn't really sure I wanted to know.

Perhaps because I had asked about the cross, or maybe just because she cared about my soul, Laura invited me to attend church with her the following Sunday. Although the cross episode definitely left a sour taste in my mouth, I still really wanted to go to church, so I asked my mom. Once again I was faced with my mother's negativity towards anything Christian. She had to draw the line somewhere. Jews attended synagogues, not churches. Jews studied the Torah, not the New Testament. Jews kept company with Jews, not *goyum*, because if you associate with Christians, you might end up marrying one—which I did, in due course.

I did not go to church with Laura that Sunday, and we never did become close friends. But I think I will remember that special classmate for the rest of my life. My time with her planted a strong desire in my heart to delve deeply into the true essence of Christianity.

A Secret Relationship

The emotional climate of the home I grew up in was fertile ground for my secret relationship with God. There was not a lot of harmony or shared affection between my parents, and my father would often walk out of the house to cool off with his friend, Ed. I was afraid that my parents would divorce, even though they were very conservative, very traditional and didn't even believe in such a thing. Still, I imagined the worst.

Since I had no spiritual mentors, I devised my own ways of seeking refuge in God. Somehow, I just knew that He was my only comfort and hope during times of distress. My bed felt like the safest and most private place in the house, and under the blankets was even more secret, so that's where I went to pour my heart out to God. I would sit up, creating a sort of "tent of meeting", and with the blankets draped over my head, I would sob and sing a song I had heard on the radio that had touched my tender soul very deeply, even though my simple little child's mind couldn't quite figure out the lyrics: *Oh sinner man, where you gonna run to, Oh sinner man, where you gonna run to... You should've been a prayin', Oh sinner man, you should've been a prayin'.*

I understood so little about anything spiritual at that immature time in my life that I actually thought the words were, *Oh cinnamon, where you gonna run to, Oh cinnamon, where you gonna run to...*, so I sang my tearful heart out, not caring at all that spices, hiding, and praying weren't usually spoken about in one breath.

Somehow, I fully believed that there was a very big God

everywhere, and that He could hear my desperate prayers and songs of yearning, and that He wanted to love me in my helplessness and emotional pain. My faith was just there from the very beginning. It was a gift from God.

Whatever the reason, I thought that if I showed the sincerity of my request by offering to sacrifice my life in exchange for my parents not getting divorced, that selfless act would be pleasing to Him. So I proposed a deal. *God, if you keep my parents from getting divorced, I will willingly die when I am forty-two years old. You can take my life then, and I will know why and be okay with that.* I felt that the deal was signed, sealed, and delivered, and I was convinced that I no longer had to police my parents' marriage. It would be protected.

Even though I didn't know anything about the character of our Creator and that He wasn't interested in plea bargaining, my faith in prayer as a means of connecting directly with Him remained strong. Prayer was all I had to see me through many years of hard times growing up. No one knew about my faith. It was a personal matter between me and the One who had become my best Friend.

Irresistible Crosses

Throughout my childhood I was very attracted to crosses. At a certain point, I decided I wanted to have one for myself. I knew I wouldn't be able to wear it in front of anyone because I was Jewish. But I figured when I was alone in my room with the door closed, I could put it around my neck, look in the mirror, and *pretend* to be a Christian. The problem was figuring out how I could actually acquire a cross. I had allowance money, but I was required to give an accounting of how I spent it, so that wasn't an option.

One day I was in the local five and dime store, several blocks from my house. I noticed a section of beautiful necklaces with cross pendants on them. I was mesmerized. I hadn't seen them before. Perhaps because it was getting close to Christmas time, the shopkeeper decided to bring in some Christian items. There was no question in my mind. I had to have at least one. So, when I knew no one was looking, I slipped a necklace into my school bag and walked out the door. My heart was beating fast and hard as I rushed passed my elementary school en route to my house, arriving there in record time.

For the next few days, I passed on playing with the neighborhood kids after school and went instead to view the array of crosses. My covetous nature had been fully aroused. I decided I wanted at least four or five of the necklaces, since some were gold, some were silver, some were plain, and some were fancy. My fascination was strong. I was thinking that the more crosses I had, the more I could experience what it was like to be a Christian. The end seemed to justify the means.

So, without even bothering to look around, I grabbed a bunch of crosses and flung them into my bag. As I headed for the door, a voice came out of nowhere, "Young lady, what do you have there in your bag?" I must have been so humiliated and terrified that I lost all consciousness of what was going on. The next thing I remember was pulling up to my lily white house in the back seat of a police car.

My parents took this episode to be a double transgression. Not only did they have a daughter who was a thief, but a traitor to her own religion as well. I had ruined the family name that my ancestors had fought so hard to maintain with honesty and integrity. Israel was mentioned somewhere in the emotional mix, and I felt myself being banished from the Promised Land, whatever that was. Much to my shock, my father encouraged the policeman to lock me up in jail and keep me there. Considering that I was only nine years old, that would have been a rather severe punishment.

Fortunately, the cop was focused on the theft part of the crime and couldn't care less about my silly, childish attempt to convert to Christianity. He suggested that my parents take me back to the store to make things right with the owner, and then follow it up with some disciplinary actions at home. This was the course that was taken. Not only did I learn a good lesson about the perils of stealing; I also came to recognize that crosses were objects that didn't have the power to give me what it was that I really wanted. I don't think I realized it at the time, but my longing was for something far deeper and far more personal. I needed a spiritual encounter, an experience that would reveal to me, without a doubt, who Jesus Christ really was.

God's Chosen

Confusion over my spiritual identity continued as I got older. As I reached my thirteenth birthday and was being prepared for bat mitzvah, I became very reflective concerning my standing with the Jewish religion. I definitely liked the idea of taking my place at the pulpit in the synagogue and leading the congregation in a special service. In all honesty, though, all I was thinking about was the stunning turquoise dress I was going to wear, and how on earth I was going to get through all the Hebrew prayers I needed to sing.

The thought of dedicating my life to God as an adult member of the Jewish community never even entered my mind. In retrospect, I imagine that the rabbi who was teaching my Hebrew class must have talked about the true purpose of my coming of age as a young Jewish woman, but none of that penetrated. Mostly, I had been sitting in the back row of the class all semester, rolling my eyes, laughing at inappropriate times, and wondering if Rabbi Cohen was as weird at home as he was at the temple.

My big day came and went with lots of fanfare and cele-bration. I thoroughly enjoyed the ceremony, with all its rituals and traditions, but I felt that something was fundamentally off. When I got real with myself, I had to admit that I just didn't relate to my whole Jewish heritage. I even felt uncomfortable being identified with Jews, although I knew as a people, Jews were generally high-minded, philanthropic, and industrious, and were considered to be chosen by God.

However, in my case, Judaism wasn't working. I yearned for a personal experience of God's love. I just couldn't feel God's heart in the Jewish religion. In fact, I didn't even know that God had a heart.

According to my very limited understanding, the God of the Jews was just a lofty concept that you somehow were supposed to believe in and celebrate by singing Hebrew songs. The truth was, I was moving farther and farther away from actual communion with God the more I tried to adopt my parents' religion.

Beyond the Mundane

As I entered junior high school, my spiritual predicament heightened. The fact that I was unable to embrace the ways and values of the world created a very real threat to my inner peace and stability. It seemed that God had wired me to think differently than many of my peers. I always had something gnawing at me, deep inside my being. I was not satisfied going through the motions of day-to-day life without probing for some profound meaning.

I observed wistfully that other girls in my classes were completely wrapped up in boys, sports, and clubs. Their lives looked so simple and fun. I admit, I certainly was boy crazy and participated in extracurricular activities too, but my soul was relentless in pondering the purpose of life beyond the visible. My connection was more to the supernatural than to the natural. This made things very difficult for me, both at home and out in the world.

One day I was in the library, and noticed a very large book that had been left out on a study table. It was "Crime and Punishment" by Fyodor Dostoevsky. I began thumbing through the pages, and stopped suddenly on this adage: "Suffering is the sole origin of consciousness." Was this philosophy? Communism? Theology? Whatever people called it, I didn't really care. I was hungry to learn more. I had a marker with me, and I very carefully wrote "suffering is the sole origin of consciousness" on my school binder notebook, taking great pains to form each letter of that meaningful statement with precision.

Compared to the typical inscriptions that my classmates sported on their binders—"Diane loves Michael," "Go Pirates!" and the like—my notebook looked pretty weird decorated with the words of a hardcore Russian author. But, I was compelled to follow my passions. My zealous nature was intense: desperate to crack the codes of life, even though I was just an adolescent. It seemed to me that mulling over the purpose of existence was far more important than anything that was going on in the school environment.

During this time period of my early teens, my mind became more and more preoccupied with basic philosophical questions. Sitting in classes, one ear would listen to the teacher, while the other was tuned into my own self-examination.

Why am I always so unhappy? Why don't I feel any love, even though I have a very good family and close friends? Will anything ever give me joy and fulfillment? Why does life seem so empty and futile? What is the purpose of school, work, families, or anything for that matter, if we're all going to end up dead at the end? Why bother?

I would ask myself these things over and over. I had lots of questions, but no answers. The school curriculum seemed trivial compared to what I was contemplating.

In my soul-searching inquiries, a divinely written song entitled "*What is the Measure of a Man?*" was given to me one evening as I sat alone in my room singing. Focusing on the importance of virtuous character rather than externals, the profound lyrics to this song let me know that God had taken hold of my heart and wasn't letting go. The innermost parts of me were crying out for something far more substantial than wondering if someone was going to step on my blue suede shoes.

"What is the measure of a man? What is the measure of a man? Not his knowledge or books, his handsome good looks; not his fortune or fame, or family name; No no, No no; It's his love and his care, his courage to dare, to know the truth, to live the truth; This is the measure, now and forever, This is the measure of a man."

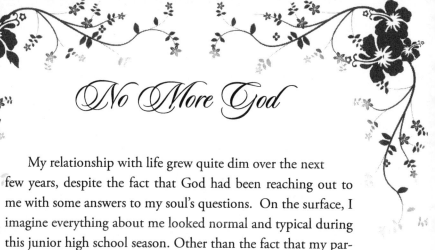

No More God

My relationship with life grew quite dim over the next few years, despite the fact that God had been reaching out to me with some answers to my soul's questions. On the surface, I imagine everything about me looked normal and typical during this junior high school season. Other than the fact that my parents thought I had an unpleasant disposition, I really doubt if anyone even sensed that I was deeply lost and miserable.

I got good grades in school, played tennis, volleyball, piano, and clarinet, and I was out in front twirling a baton in parades. One would think I would have experienced a certain amount of satisfaction. Quite the contrary, I felt very sad and bereft almost all the time. There was a lot of talk in school about the Soviet Union wanting to attack the U.S., and I knew in my heart of hearts that I hoped they would. Total annihilation of life as I knew it was the only solution I could see for my existential angst.

I don't remember what happened to the intimate prayer life I had when I was younger, but somehow, it just disappeared. My reliance on prayer must have been a slow fade, because the fact that I stopped praying *altogether* never became an issue for me.

By the time I was in high school, I no longer turned to God for help at all. In fact, I completely stopped believing in God. What made sense to me was that the human condition was so filled with suffering, that in this horrible predicament, man made up the existence of God to cajole himself into feeling better. That was my distorted belief for a season: that man created God as an escape from reality.

I remember someone asking me during this high school period if I believed in God, and I said "no" without any hesitation. Then he asked me if I was an agnostic or an atheist. After listening to the definitions he gave, that an agnostic was someone who would be open to believing in God if His existence could be proven, and that an atheist was someone who definitely would not believe in God, no matter what, I decided that I was an atheist. No one was going to prove anything to me. God was a figment of man's imagination, and that was that!

My defiant, ungodly attitude sent up red flags for my folks, so for my high school graduation gift, mom and dad decided to fly me to the Motherland for one month to put some religion back in me. They figured that time in Israel would connect me to my Jewish roots and heritage, and get me back on track. Since I had no interest in traveling with any kind of group, I asked my best friend Lesley to accompany me on what our parents had determined would be an inspiring, soul-correcting pilgrimage.

"*Shalom! Shalom!*" a father-and-son looking team greeted us joyfully as Lesley and I claimed our suitcases in Tel Aviv and looked around for a bus. The two men were both smiling from ear to ear and speaking excitedly in their native language, as they concocted some kind of plan that seemed to focus on us. *Had our contact person sent these guys to meet us at the airport? Why didn't they at least have a note written in English explaining what was going on? Our instructions were to take a bus into the city to find our lodging. What did these men want?*

Before Lesley and I could figure out what was happening, our volunteer hosts grabbed our luggage and ushered us onto an extremely crowded bus. Clearing away a group of young locals who were dominating the back of the public vehicle, the two men with our suitcases secured one seat for us to share.

The father figure then lifted his voice above the regular traveling din and apparently asked the bus riders, "Is there an interpreter in the house?" This question set off a few seconds of friendly talking amongst all the passengers. The whole busload of local Israelis seemed to already know each other. Finally, a middle aged man explained to us in very broken English that we were being escorted to the family home of our hosts, where we would be their honored guests. The whole chain of events from the moment we had landed at the Tel Aviv airport was our unofficial Israeli welcome.

After a very unsettling and strangely entertaining ride, we arrived at a tiny apartment in a crowded village. A woman appeared from the simple dwelling with two young children. These three unsuspecting people were also part of our unofficial welcoming committee.

After removing our luggage from the bus, our Hebrew escorts began rearranging the living quarters so that their whole family of five could camp out on the living room floor. Lesley and I were given the only bedroom. We were dumbfounded. These people didn't know us from Adam, they couldn't speak a word of English to connect with us verbally, and yet they brought us into their private sanctuary and gave us the best that they had. I got the sense that shalom meant more than just "hello," "goodbye," and "peace." The Israeli spirit was over-whelmingly warm, sacrificial, and intimate.

The following day, Lesley and I bid our hosts farewell and

31

in earnest began our sightseeing trip around the country. We visited all the standard tourist places, and although there certainly was a great deal of Israeli history wherever we went, we found the whole experience to be mundane and boring. The people continued to be welcoming, which was kind of fun, but truthfully, we couldn't figure out what the big deal was about Israel, and why our parents wanted to send us there. True, we were both more conscious of our Jewishness on what was considered by others to be holy ground, but so what? A trip to the Bahamas would have been a much better choice, as far as we were concerned.

A few days before my friend and I returned home, I had an encounter with a being that sent me reeling. I woke up in the middle of the night and went into the bathroom of our cheap hotel room. As I turned on the light, something moved very quickly behind the bathtub. Thoughts flew through my mind, *What is that? It's humongous. It's got webbed feet, bulging eyes, a long, whipping tail, and scaly skin. There is no way that God would ever make such a horrendous creature. That thing has got to be a mistake—a freak of nature! Forget the synagogues, holy books, and rituals. The Jews must be blind. All they have to do is look around. If there were a God, He wouldn't think up such insane ways to amuse Himself.*

Whatever "religion" that my parents thought would rub off on me in Israel didn't. In fact, when Lesley and I returned to the United States, I was more convinced than ever that man had created God. As far as I was concerned, there was just as much evidence that God was dead as that He was alive and well.

Visionless Academia

By the time I went off to college in upstate New York, the spiritual dilemmas that had beset me in my younger days were completely gone. There was nothing to ruminate about any more. I no longer cared about anything enough to try to make sense out of it. With no vision whatsoever for my future, I would have perished on my own. But since my parents were paying for my education, I followed their plans for my life. Mom and Dad wanted me to become a high school English teacher, so that's the course I followed.

University life was my last-ditch attempt to find something in this world that I could sink my teeth into. As it turned out, college level academics weren't really my cup of tea, so I spent as much time as I could smoking cigarettes and marijuana, drinking alcohol, having casual sex, performing folk-singing gigs at a popular club, and eating at restaurants with my roommate, perfecting the poor-college-student art of "dine and dash." With nothing to call me higher than figuring out how to simultaneously use the system and drop out of it, I sunk deeper and deeper into darkness.

My college friends were engaged in the same kinds of activities that I was, but they all seemed to respond very differently to everything than I did. Whatever my cohorts indulged in gave them pleasure—albeit temporary—but at least they were experiencing fun and happiness exploring this and that. In my case, everything I engaged in magnified the torment of my soul. Getting high on pot exaggerated my feelings of isolation and despair, and having sex always ended up with me in a pool of hot, salty tears, and the guy wondering what in the world just happened. I didn't know what was wrong with these common extra-curricular activities, but I knew *something* was really wrong. No matter what I did, the result was always sorrow and confusion.

West Coast Religion

My outlook on life radically changed when I began consistently dating one of my classmates. Immediately smiles appeared on my face, and laughter burst forth from my heart. Robert and I finished our undergraduate studies together, got married, and moved to San Francisco, where my young husband attended law school (according to his parents' plans), and I became a high school English teacher (according to my parents' plans).

The Haight-Ashbury hippie phenomenon was in full swing when we arrived at the Golden Gate. I felt as if I had moved to a different planet, not just a different state! Brightly dressed flower children were everywhere, proclaiming love to be *it*. Whatever the question, love was the answer. I was fascinated. With all the darkness and confusion I had lived with for so much of my life, I had no idea that there was such a profound and simple solution to everything.

Not only were the hippies talking about, singing about, and acting out love, as they knew it, but they were very committed to making sure that this love was free—free love. That was the sum and substance of their message. But what exactly was free love?

As far as I could tell, free love was about first loving yourself and then sharing that love unabashedly with others. Sex, drugs, and rock and roll, the "religion" of the day on the West Coast, were the channels through which that love was being expressed.

Robert and I lived double lives for quite some time. During the week we continued on our straight paths as law student and high school teacher, and on the weekends we got stoned out of our minds, and danced with wild abandon at love-ins. Naturally, the weekend activities started leaking into our professional lives. Something had to give.

My husband and I decided to step out of the tight boxes that we were in, which really represented our parents' values and visions, not ours. We made a plunge into the metaphysical. Robert quit law school with less than one semester to go; I quit my teaching job, and both of us turned our attentions inward. There was every kind of self-revelatory hallucinogen known to man in San Francisco, and we didn't even have to go looking for them. They came to us! So off we went into the world of psychedelics, ostensibly seeking truth and God.

I actually did see God on one LSD trip, or so I thought, in my delusional state. I was on the beach at Half Moon Bay, gazing up at the sky, when all of a sudden the clouds turned into the most exquisite sight I had ever seen. The colors were other-worldly; scintillatingly gorgeous. The majesty of it all took my breath away. *Finally*, I said out loud to myself and the universe, *I have found God in all His glory. He really does exist!!*

The only problem was, in order to re-experience this counterfeit glory of God and continue to believe in His existence, I had to keep taking psychedelics, which I did. Robert was not having the same kind of "revelations" that I was, so he was not so motivated to drop every pill down his throat that came along unbidden from "angels who just wanted to share the love."

A part of me was getting concerned that I was becoming a drug addict, but I was always assured by the self-appointed psychedelic aficionados not to worry. It was only the hard drugs, dark substances like heroin and speed that were addictive. The love drugs were medicine. The reason you always wanted more was because they were good for you. This was the theory of the day, which I readily accepted.

As I became more and more absorbed in tripping out to other dimensions on my own, and Robert remained somewhat grounded hoping to find a real direction for his life, my young husband and I drifted very far apart. He wasn't interested in my out-of-body experiences and I wasn't interested in any of his in-the-body experiences. There was very little common ground left between us, and neither one of us had any understanding about the sacredness of the marriage vows we had taken. So, it was just a matter of time before we got to the point of an inevitable divorce.

One final joint adventure together was a night out on the town. Robert and I went to see the musical play "Hair." We sat next to three very interesting people who were really eager to share their drugs with us. Truly, this sharing of drugs at large public events was the underlying glue that kept the hippie culture together for so long. Joints, powders, and pills were passed around to total strangers to create one body, one mind, and one spirit in the gathering hall. This was the free love phenomenon. Our hearts and minds blended together. The message became clear to me before the night was over. It was time for me to get serious about my spiritual quest and stop dabbling. I was ready to turn on, tune in, and drop out.

It took me a few days to figure out how I was going to break the news to Robert that I wanted to end our marriage. Since the emotional bond between us had already eroded at such a deep level, and the only feelings I could summon up were drug-induced agonies and ecstasies which couldn't be translated into words, I decided not to speak to my husband face-to-face. I was going to leave him the car and all our possessions and assets except the money I had saved up from my teaching job, so I figured he might not even be that upset if I just took off and left him a note. That's what I did.

With a large suitcase in hand, a supply of mind-altering psychedelic drugs in my purse, and no thoughts beyond tomorrow, I hitch-hiked across the Golden Gate Bridge to my new life in Marin. For six months, I stayed there with an unlikely cast of characters whom I met quite randomly. This included Carole, a psychic and tarot card reader, Edwin, a defected FBI agent, Justin, a psychedelic artist who had inherited a large family fortune, Melanie, an avid follower of the Sufi order, and Kent, a good-looking but very messed up speed addict and drug dealer. By the end of six months, I decided I'd had enough of northern California and the hippie scene, so I sold some of my fine jewelry and bought a one-way ticket to Maui.

Pursuing the Mastermind

As the plane hit ground in Kahului, Maui, an inspiring, purposeful feeling enveloped my entire being. I sensed that I was not coming to Hawaii as a tourist. I was a pilgrim. The pervasive scent of Plumeria flowers in the air and the beautiful, majestic scenery provided the perfect backdrop for a fresh start in my relentless pursuit. My heart began to sing. *God is here, and I am going to find Him!* I was definitely still empty, but hopeful.

Leaving the airport, I literally didn't know whether to turn to the right or to the left, to head for the hills or towards the ocean. I faced the sunshine and stuck out my thumb. The driver who picked me up turned out to be from the same small town where I had grown up in the suburbs of New York. In fact, his brother and I had been classmates. What an outrageous coincidence!

I became immediately convinced that there was a Mastermind, an all-knowing God, who had orchestrated and designed this wonderful meeting. I determined to find out who that Genius beyond all geniuses was, and why He arranged unexplainable coincidences. *Was it to give evidence of His existence? Was it to give us faith that we are being watched over and taken care of?* From that very obvious divine appointment on, I truly understood that I was never alone. The Friend I used to pray to when I was much younger was as omnipresent and omniscient as ever. He was always with me and directing my wanderings, even though I had chosen to ignore Him so much of the time.

My adventure continued to a popular waterfall, where I met an assortment of very zealous Christians. Perhaps they were just sincerely trying to share the gospel, but in the state I was in, steeped in darkness and confusion, I found their less-than-personal interest in me really annoying. They pounded and pounded the Word, pointing to Bible verses as they preached, and I just became more and more bewildered trying to follow them. I couldn't tell what they were trying to teach me. *Love? Sin? Lamb of God? Messiah? Repentance? Forgiveness? Salvation?*

These young evangelical Christians obviously knew I was very lost, but what they didn't know was how to reach me. Perhaps they neglected to call upon the Holy Spirit to minister to me, or perhaps my soul just wasn't ready to have the spiritual truths unlocked. The unfortunate result was that I left their company with the clear intention of staying as far away from Christians as possible in the future.

I had already had my fill of Jews in New York, hippies in California, and now Christians on Maui. There really wasn't anyone I could relate to very well, and anyway, I thought it would just be easier and more peaceful to keep to myself. Dealing with people seemed to be more trouble than it was worth. So I lived in a tent alone on a gorgeous beach until the tent got stolen. From there, I moved into a cave. The dampness and darkness left much to be desired, but there was a lot to be said for location, location, location. I had a multi-million dollar view of the ocean, the mountains, and a small island off in the distance.

Although I kept a very low profile during this cave dwelling period, I did work at a lunch café a few days a week—that is, until my double-life of work and recreational drugs came into conflict once again, as it had in San Francisco. There was absolutely no contest this time, when I set both values side-by-side. I hadn't come all that way to the Hawaiian Islands to whip up smoothies and sandwiches for tourists and get paid slightly more than minimum wage. Maui-wowee won out, hands down.

The higher I got on the locally grown *pakalolo* (Hawaiian cannabis), the more restless my soul became. There I was in a virtual paradise, and still feeling deep inside my heart as if I was camping out at the gates of hell. Aside from smoking some-thing or ingesting something, I had no idea how to seek God. I longed to be in His presence, and to feel at home in Him. I was exhausted and depleted from all the sorrows and meaning-lessness of my life. There was absolutely nothing to show for all I had been through.

Desperate for some profound answers to life's most painful, unanswered questions, I decided maybe it was time to seek out a spiritual guru. Not that I even knew exactly what a guru was, but the whole idea of the master/disciple relationship really appealed to me. *India! Maybe that's the next step—a sojourn to India to find a guru.*

A Supernatural Deliverance

A few days after I began thinking about a possible trip to India, a group of Hindu Krishna devotees came to the beach where I was staying, to share their faith. They were chanting, dancing, and talking about God, their guru, and discipleship. Although they were Americans, most of them had spent time in India with their guru. This was what I was looking for, or so I thought.

The devotees invited me to visit their *ashram*, a simple but beautiful monastery in the jungle. My whole experience there was very weird. I could barely relate to anything that was going on. I wasn't clear if the monastic lifestyle and Hindu values were the problem, or if I was the problem. As I searched inwardly for the answer, I thought, *I can only take this in small doses. Maybe I'll come again, but for now, I need to get out of here.*

The journey back to my cave on the beach from the Hindu ashram was much more than I bargained for. I began hitchhiking shortly before dusk. An old station wagon soon stopped to pick me up. As I looked inside, I saw only two very large men who appeared to have just come from a luau. I had not had any personal contact with the locals before, but I imagined that they would all have delightful aloha spirits. *They'll probably serenade me with sweet Hawaiian music all the way down the road. This is going to be fun!*

What a "rude awakening" I received! As I got into the

back seat, a third younger man, who had been lying down to obscure his presence, sat up and started pulling me in. A terrifying, demonic-sounding laughter enveloped me as I fell into the vehicle. The door shut. I was imprisoned. This hell trap on wheels made its way through the endless sugar cane fields, alongside the even more endless ocean. I was completely disoriented and absolutely mortified.

Then the station wagon came to a halt. "You make 'a one sound, and you be dead. You see that big ocean ova there, huh? That's where you be for a very long time, and no one find you. You hear?" I did hear. These definitely were not empty threats. The thought occurred to me that I probably should have ended my depraved life by suicide before this event. At least that way, I would have been able to determine the method of my own death.

Each one of the intoxicated Hawaiians took two turns at raping me. I did not move or utter a sound. What happened during these atrocities was an absolute miracle of divine grace. The Lord Jesus Christ showed up personally and protected me from the trauma. His presence became more real to me than the obscene perpetration that was taking place. I literally felt that Jesus lifted me (my inner being) up above my body, gently held me, and allowed me to be a witness to the violence that was taking place, without actually being a victim to it. This was especially miraculous, because I didn't even believe in Jesus at the time.

As one would expect, considering the intensity of this whole experience, some very important spiritual truths were revealed to me. Firstly, I became aware beyond a shadow of a doubt that I was loved and protected by an all-seeing God. Secondly, I discovered that the Lord's peace could cover any situation, no matter how terrifying and violent. *I felt completely safe and cared for the entire time I was being raped.* Even though my flesh was being savagely abused, resting in Jesus was sufficient to bring deep peace to my heart and soul. Thirdly, I learned about the all-consuming nature of lust, and how it can turn men into repulsive animals if it was not kept in check. Fourthly, I learned about the Savior's forgiveness.

Although I did not hear the words *"Father, forgive them, for they know not what they do"* (Luke 2:34), I felt the essence of those gracious words down to the core of my being. This supernatural spirit of love was put inside me. It was the refuge for my soul. As such, I was able to walk away from the rape with absolutely no anger, resentment, or desire for retaliation: only a heart of compassion.

In retrospect, it's hard for me to imagine how I could have gone through this radical event and not fallen on my knees asking Jesus to be the Lord of my life, but that is not what happened. I received His amazing miracle of grace as a matter of course, and just returned to my crazy self-guided life exactly the way it was. The only thing that changed was my physical well-being: I had contracted a venereal disease from the rapists.

The Hindu Monastery

Fasting and praying out in nature had been a regular part of my lifestyle for some time, and I decided to try to purge the venereal disease out of my body by eating a light fruit diet for a couple of weeks. I found a private place where I could be alone with God, unclothed, and unfed.

It was on the third day of my fast that I was jarred out of my meditations by two policemen who were standing right in front of me, out in the middle of nowhere. They did not speak, but just stared at my naked body. I thought I must be hallucinating. *You're just paranoid. There are no policemen here. You're alone with God.* I closed my eyes, returning to my inner place of solitude.

Once again, I sensed an intrusion. Opening my eyes, I saw one of the officers motioning to my clothes, as the other one spoke. "You are under arrest for indecent exposure." Apparently, the remote valley I had picked out from a topographical map wasn't as hidden as I thought. A tourist had spotted me from a lookout point and called the authorities. These two cops were taking me to jail as soon as I got dressed.

I tried to explain that I meant no harm to anyone. I was just trying to be very close to God and have Him heal my body, which had been victimized and defiled. *Why aren't the cops more interested in finding and arresting the rapists than bothering me? Why doesn't the law protect the gentle and go after the violent?* I expressed my broken heart in vain. I might as well have been speaking Greek.

These local police were not much friendlier to me than the local rapists. They treated me as a common criminal, reading me no rights whatsoever. After dumping out the contents of my purse on a table, they pushed me into a filthy, dark holding cell. It was the size of a small closet, and looked and smelled like it purposely hadn't been cleaned for years. All of my anti-establishment values were intensified. It was clear to me that the government was fundamentally heartless. These guys couldn't tell the difference between a nature-loving pilgrim and a murderer, or if they could tell the difference, they just didn't care. Everyone got treated as the lowest of the low.

I had no idea how long I would have to stay in that cell, or what it would take to get out. The officers told me nothing. After my initial panic subsided, I noticed that the dirty walls were covered with writing. There were many handwritten verses from the *Bhagavad Gita*, the main Hindu holy book, apparently written by a previous cell occupant. I read the verses with relish, learning for the very first time some fundamental spiritual truths that rocked my soul. These teachings were all I had to cling on to, and I decided if I ever got out of jail, I would return to the Hindu ashram and delve into the Vedic scriptures.

Several hours later I was suddenly released from the dark, smelly cell. I was told that a girl from the Hindu ashram just happened to see the police going after someone in the not-so-hidden valley, and wondered what was going on. She called the police station, found out my identity, and put up bail for me. The chances of something like this happening were so far-fetched that obviously, something mystical was going on. I was completely blown away. It seemed that God was trying to get to me through those Hindu people. There was no ques-

46

tion about it. The next day I returned to the ashram to see if I could get a grip on everything that had taken place.

Once again, as I reentered the monastery world, I felt like a stranger in a strange land. I was faced with culture shock at every turn. But I figured if millions and millions of people could buy into this religion, it must be for real. So, I kept my mind open.

On the positive side, I found myself very drawn to the spiritual doctrines of the Hindu religion. Most of the teachings sounded like profound truth, and whatever didn't, I figured would, over time. I also really enjoyed the chanting and dancing, which I experienced as a beautiful celebration of God's love. And the gourmet vegetarian food was off the charts! I had never tasted anything so delicious in my life.

But on the flip side, there were aspects of Hinduism that I found quite appalling. There was serious idol worship going on. Of course, the Krishna devotees told me that these were not idols, but deities; that God Himself who had no limits, agreed to come down into those figures to help us relate to Him personally, but I found the whole experience very, very strange.

I couldn't help but wince when the devotees bowed down and prostrated themselves before what seemed to me to be elaborately dressed dolls. They certainly were beautiful, carved marble dolls, but I could feel nothing in their presence except the weirdness of assuming that was 'God' on the altar. Again, I told myself if I kept at it, over time hopefully I would become pure enough to realize that the deities were truly 'God.'

Also, a problem for me was the predominant mood of the devotees. Most of them seemed to do and say exactly the right things; the protocols and etiquette were remarkable. However,

I felt no personal love coming out of anyone, either towards me or towards each other.

The Hindu books spoke of love; the Hindu songs sang of love. All the externals were perfect, but I did not feel any real love in their temple—not that I knew what love was, I might add. I knew what love wasn't, and the pervading atmosphere at the monastery felt like what love wasn't. Certainly there was a great deal of light, but no real warmth or intimacy.

Even after participating in a service that lasted a few hours, I would go away with an unfulfilled longing in my heart. I had not felt the penetrating quality of God's love. The palpable experience that is described in Psalm 34:8, *"Oh, taste and see that the Lord is good"* was definitely missing for me.

Despite my reservations and concerns about the ashram, I decided to dive in head first. I have always been radical and intense in my pursuits, and this was no exception. I figured it would be worth a few months of my practically useless life to live as a monastic nun. If I didn't like it, I would just leave. This was going to be a short experiment—no big deal.

The requirements for moving into the monastery were crystal clear. Four primary vows that had to be taken: 1) No eating of meat, fish, or eggs; 2) no sex outside of marriage, and within marriage only once a month for procreation; 3) no intoxication including stimulants (coffee, tea, chocolate, etc.); 4) no gambling, idle entertainment (including TV), and mental speculation. It was a lot to commit to, but I was serious about finding the truth, at all costs. At that time, I believed that taking these vows was a necessary first step to approaching God. This was a fundamental teaching of the guru, Swami Prabhupada.

In addition to the don'ts, there were the dos. Daily ashram life was completely regulated by *tapas*; austerities meant to subdue the flesh and strengthen the spirit. Each morning the devotees would greet the day with an Indian style reveille, wake the cells up with a three minute cold shower, dress in fresh, clean temple attire, and show up in the temple at 4 a.m. for several hours of chanting, dancing, and Vedic study.

Breakfast was then served for all those who had been diligent and faithful enough to participate in the entire morning devotional. Occasionally, someone would slip through the cracks and be served the delicious hot cereal and fruit alongside the more stalwart devotees, but for the most part, if you were too sick and tired to worship and study at 4 a.m., you were too sick and tired to eat at 7 a.m. Because I loved both the discipline and the food, I never went without either.

Following the breakfast meal, each of us would go directly back to our meager living quarters, clean our personal spaces to a standard of "cleanliness is next to godliness" perfection, and get ready for the day's work. Uplifting, joyful music pervaded the atmosphere as we performed our tasks which not only energized us, but kept the devotees from engaging in any frivolous, mundane conversations. Social relationships just for the purpose of getting to know one another's personalities were kept to a minimum. Unless you were going to talk about Krishna or the guru and his world-wide mission, you were admonished to zip your lips.

The day's activities varied for the devotees according to our talents and propensities. As in any community, there were the standard jobs—cooks, cleaners, builders, treasurers, teachers, doctors. In addition, because this was a vibrant religious organization, there were also proselytizers and fund-raisers. I found myself naturally drawn to be a part of the missionary group because of a fiery zeal that burned in my bones. I just couldn't sit still or keep my mouth shut. My mother said I was born that way. No matter what I was excited about, I fully believed that everyone else should be excited about it too. In this case, my daily passion was directed toward converting people to the Hare Krishna sect of Hinduism.

My intense workdays out on the field proselytizing and raising funds were sandwiched between morning and evening devotionals. Not one day went by in the 20 years that I lived as a monastic nun that I skimped on the spiritual disciplines. I considered it my duty as well as my privilege and joy to worship, pray, and study very diligently before eating breakfast, and before "taking rest" at night.

Vedic understanding associated sleep with ignorance and death, so my nightly experience of lying down on a simple mat on the floor became a conscious, intentional act of resting, not a careless succumbing to a dark force. Cushy king and queen-sized beds were viewed as traps of *Maya* (the Hindu version of Satan). "Bare-bones" was the rule of the monastery, and I will say that after many years of sleeping on the hard floor, my bones *were* actually becoming bare. So I allowed myself to upgrade to a thin mattress. The provisions for the flesh when I was in my 40's were different than they were when I was in my 20's, but the principle remained the same: *Less is more.* Less bodily identification meant more spiritual focus.

All of this dynamic spiritual boot camp training proved highly profitable in my life for years to come, for which I am very grateful. However, there were also some unwelcome emotional, physical, and spiritual side effects to this unbalanced, arduous lifestyle that took their toll on me.

At the very beginning of my ashram life, I realized that I didn't want to have anything to do with the regular outside world. After a few years, even if I had wanted to mingle, I wouldn't have known how. This became very apparent to my parents who were deeply concerned for my well-being.

One day, my mother and father showed up at the monastery, ostensibly to take me to a shopping mall. My relationship with my parents had always been strained, with worlds of differences between us, so I assumed they were just trying to find a way to spend time together that wouldn't set off a major disagreement.

Stepping into the back seat of Mom and Dad's Oldsmobile, I was immediately overwhelmed with a very weird feeling and lots of emotionally charged thoughts. *Why did I agree to go with them? What business do I have shopping at a worldly mall, anyway? I hate the world and its entrapments. All that stuff in the stores is useless to me. I already have everything I need. God naturally provides it. Why stimulate unnecessary desires?* I couldn't come up with any good reasons to relax and enjoy myself in my parents' company.

As the car headed towards the mall, I noticed that my father was creeping very slowly along the road, driving 10mph in a 25mph speed zone. The brownstone houses we passed were pretty ordinary looking, so it certainly wasn't the scenery that was setting the drawn out pace. I sensed a cold, quiet, uptight mood in the car that I couldn't quite identify, but didn't like. *Can't he hurry up and just get to the mall already? This is taking way too long. I have important service to perform back at the ashram!* I could feel my heart begin to race, as if attempting to propel the vehicle forward with more oomph and purpose.

My father was the first to break the uncomfortable silence. A rapid fire of suspicion-laden questions came pouring out into the back seat, where I was sitting with a flimsy posture, trying to be somewhat invisible: "Why do the men shave their heads? Why don't the women speak up? Why do the children live with their teachers, and not with their parents? Why don't you at least eat a little fish? Where are you getting your protein from? Why don't you stay in touch with your brother and sister?"

Then my mother chimed in with her uninformed, but genuine concerns: "How come the guru sits on an elevated platform? Why do you have to get up at 3 a.m.? What's wrong with getting a good night's sleep? Why do they send you out on the streets to proselytize? Have you forgotten that you're Jewish? Why have you abandoned your own religion? Why aren't you allowed to visit your family whenever you want to? " *Oh no! This feels like the Salem witch trials! And, they don't even want to know the real answers. If I tell her I **am** allowed to visit my family as often as I want to, she'll go even crazier. There's no way out of this.*

Finally the questioning reached a pitch where my mother could no longer contain her tears or the volume of her voice. "Sam, I can't do it! I'm not going through with this. That deprogrammer is awful. We can't put our daughter in his hands! He even smelled terrible."

What?? My parents met with some religious cult deprogrammer? They must have hired him to "rescue" me. Are they attempting to kidnap me right now? Is this their distorted idea of love? I'm getting out of here! They don't love me. They don't even know who I am!

As the car slowed down to turn a corner, I flung open the door, jumped out, and started running full speed ahead towards the ashram.

I had heard about quite a few people from different spiritual paths—Buddhists, Catholics, Protestants, Hindus, Jesus freaks—who had been kidnapped by their family members and brought to the most well-known deprogrammer at the time.

Somehow, this man was able to convince many people to allow the use of horrendous torture methods to win their "loved ones" over to a different way of thinking. Sleep deprivation, starvation, screaming obscenities at people, forcing meat down vegetarians' throats, parading naked women in front of celibate monks, and other atrocious techniques were used to wear people down and brain-wash them into thinking the way whoever was paying the bill was thinking.

Obviously, my parents didn't know their own daughter at all. My mind and my heart were not up for grabs. I was not about to be coerced into anything by human (or in this case, inhuman) means. It would take a supernatural act of God to change me from the inside out. As far as I was concerned, I had made a commitment to my guru, and had forsaken all other spiritual paths, not only for the rest of this lifetime, but for all eternity.

Arriving back at the ashram exhausted from running with improper shoes, I sank to my knees in gratitude that I had escaped the trap my parents had set for me. The ashram, with all its imperfections, was still very much my refuge.

My Arranged Marriage

When I first entered the ashram in 1969, I was single. The only other unmarried women were either newcomers like myself, or those rare celibates who were content to remain unencumbered by household life. The marriages that took place within the ashram were arranged either by the guru himself, or by his appointed leaders.

Sometime around my twenty-sixth birthday, I was matched up with a very prominent, extraordinarily gifted monk. This young man who became my betrothed, had been told by our guru to remain celibate for four years and then to get married. His four years were up, and I was completely ready for marriage at that time.

Rembrandt, as he was called endearingly because he painted almost exactly like the great master, (we believed that the soul reincarnated from one life time to the next, carrying talents and accomplishments in the DNA, so according to our beliefs, this man could very well have been the reincarnation of Rembrandt) spent almost all of his time, when he wasn't studying or worshiping, in front of his easel or up on a scaffold producing museum quality masterpieces.

Because the idea to marry was not Rembrandt's but the guru's, and the idea to marry me was not his own but the ashram president's, very little bonding took place between us. I felt privileged to be able to personally serve this world-class prodigy, but the truth was, as a woman and a wife, I felt completely neglected and unloved. Deep dissatisfaction was brewing inside me.

"Remember, nothing is going to change when we get married" were the most memorable words Rembrandt had spoken to me during our two month courtship, and although I had kind of gotten the gist of my fiancé's vision for our life together, I didn't realize that "nothing" actually meant *nothing*! So, in accordance with my new husband's (and our guru's) idea of the optimum situation for our marriage, Rembrandt and I continued to live separately in the monastic dormitories most of the time.

We did try living together for a short period, but when Rembrandt became distracted from his art, and I started pulling on him for a worldly kind of romance, that physical joining together as one came to an unhappy end. Our guru was getting the short end of the stick with us functioning as a traditionally married couple, and neither of us was content. So we returned to Rembrandt's original plan of keeping things the way they were before we got married. My deepest yearnings to experience my humanity full-on as a beautiful and desirable woman, not just as a selfless servant, were folded up and stuffed away. On my thirtieth birthday, I had to face myself head on. My emotional stuffing process was collapsing. I was in a major panic.

Whenever I saw other devotee women who looked fulfilled, especially those with children, I became extremely envious and jealous. It was hard to admit, but I actually hoped in my heart of hearts that something awful would happen to those families. *Was I becoming some kind of wicked witch? Where did all this uncontrollable jealousy come from?* Something was terribly wrong. Here I was in a monastery, devoting my life to God in every way that I could, yet my inner world was tormented with envy. I knew I needed help.

After several weeks of intensive prayers, but not receiving any relief from my ill-feelings, I went to an ashram elder for counsel. I confessed everything that had been going on inside me. His simple response pointed me in the right direction. "There's nothing wrong with you." Jaya das assured me. "You just need to have your own family." Fortunately, Rembrandt and I could both see the wisdom in this counsel, and together, we made a plan to have a child and create a home environment for ourselves. Before that, however, my husband wanted to send me off to India for six months to learn from the Indian women how to become an ideal submissive wife.

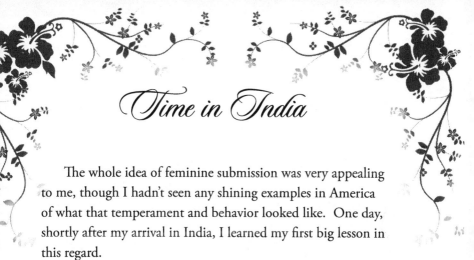

Time in India

The whole idea of feminine submission was very appealing to me, though I hadn't seen any shining examples in America of what that temperament and behavior looked like. One day, shortly after my arrival in India, I learned my first big lesson in this regard.

My friend Vara and I went to a women's bathing *ghat* (spot) at the Ganges River to cool off from the 120 degree weather. We quickly shed our *saris* (wrap-around dresses) and *cholis* (blouses) and nonchalantly tossed them on the ground. There was no one else in sight.

When Vara and I emerged from the river, a couple of hours later, our clothing had been washed, dried, and folded neatly for us. A flower had been placed on top of the impeccably stacked up items. I was astonished. The women who had performed this wonderful act of service didn't even stick around to be thanked for what they had done. They obviously had something else in mind.

I could almost hear Rembrandt shouting to me from across the seas: *Make sure you get this! This is the heart of feminine submission. It always looks for ways to humbly bless others, wanting nothing in return.*

This was only a part of an all-pervading mood of behind-the-scenes femininity that really intrigued me. The interesting thing was that I couldn't quite put my finger on what the Indian women were doing to create this air of feminine submission, what the men were doing to reinforce it, and why it all seemed so natural. I was struck by some obvious signs of a very different culture than what I was accustomed to in the West, particularly the very bold, overstated atmosphere of Los Angeles, where I was living at the time.

One thing that initially put me off was the practice of women walking several steps behind their husbands. From a typical western viewpoint, this appeared to be male chauvinism parading itself very proudly. But as I observed the relaxed pace of the women and the rather dignified and contented manner in which they talked about this dynamic, I was humbled. These ladies were not in any way feeling dishonored or unloved. In fact, they were more than happy to follow their male leaders, out on the streets, and also at home. The secondary, submissive role seemed inborn in the Indian woman's psyche. They weren't *trying* to be in the supporting role, they just were.

The preciousness of the women was exalted to the status of the back-room jewels. By remaining a step or two in the background, the women were lifted up.

Everything was going along very well with my studies and observations concerning man/woman dynamics. I noticed that my perspective was changing. It didn't have to be a struggle to live as the helpmate. I was really excited about the fresh attitude that I was developing, until I learned about the Sati rite.

The Sati rite was radical. It took feminine submission way too far, in my opinion. Just hearing about this ceremony gave me an inkling of why the Hindu-based Indian culture might be drowning in poverty, violence, disease, and other major afflictions. Something was fundamentally distorted in the principles these people were following.

According to the Sati rite, which had been an integral part

of the Indian society for many centuries past, if the husband died first, the wife would voluntarily throw herself onto her husband's funeral pyre. The reasoning was that the emotional and spiritual pain of separation would be far greater than the physical pain of death by fire.

Although I was certainly inspired by the total devotion that was the underlying principle of this Sati ritual, the whole ordeal struck me as being way over the top. *Couldn't the women pull themselves together after losing their husbands and go on with their lives? Had they disappeared to such an extent in their submissive roles that they had no identities other than as wives? Was this really God's design for man and woman? Was I willing to become like melted butter on toast that was so absorbed by my husband that his demise would automatically mean my physical death as well?*

Back Together

My calendar was marked for six months from the time I set foot on Indian soil. On the appointed day of my return, I arrived at LAX airport eager to reunite with Rembrandt. Our meeting was unpredictably tense. All I remember from our brief time together at the airport were these five painful words: "You came back too soon." Apparently I hadn't changed enough in India. We hadn't even gotten out of baggage claim, and already my husband had discovered that I was the same old saucy me.

Despite our mutual disappointment that I hadn't magically become the quiet, serenely reposed archetype Rembrandt hoped to see, my husband did stay true to his word that we would try to have a child upon my return home. We scheduled the elaborate all-day-long conception ceremonies and rituals for the optimum time of month.

Two months later, repeating the same extensive, very specific rituals, designed to "call in a spiritually mature soul," I did become pregnant. As my belly was growing, so were the monastery ranks. A new wave of enthusiasm for spreading the Krishna religion had hit the ashram. Thousands of devotees had been sent out on to the streets going everywhere there were lots of people, in an attempt to make disciples for our guru. My spirit got swept up in that wave.

Although I did not have much of a social aspect to my personality and especially shied away from crowds, this situation was different. There was a pressing need that far outweighed my introverted bent.

By the seventh month of my pregnancy, the front lines were where I yearned to be. In the secret chamber of my heart, I wished that I was not going to be tied down at home with a baby so soon. When I got real with myself, I was not someone who could be a stay-at-home mom. The way I was wired, fully plugged into the sufferings of humanity at large, I felt like I had to be out on the streets, right in the midstream of the multitudes. Being a mother would simply be an encumbrance.

On the Road Again

"She didn't make it, dear," a stoic nurse told me quite cold-
ly, as she bundled up my flesh and blood and carried the tiny
little infant out of the hospital room. The doctor could find
no medical explanation for the still birth. I was confused. *Was
God responding to my deepest desires to put family life aside so that
I could travel and preach? Was I being lifted out of my commitment to motherhood?*

It took me about a month to recuperate from the physical
and emotional pain of the delivery. One day, I realized I was
finished convalescing and grieving. I purchased a business
suit, enlisted a willing female partner, and stepped out into the
world. Operating at break-neck speed, we went wherever people congregated—museums, concerts, rodeos, parades, super
bowls, tourist towns, airports—to spread the religion that had
given our lives meaning.

Every day I approached hundreds of people, distributing
my guru's translations and commentaries on the Vedas, and
collecting donations for our soup kitchens, women's shelters,
and Krishna temples. Thousands of books flew out of my bag,
and large sums of money flew into my hands during the two
decades that I immersed myself in this very passionate and
fruitful activity.

Mixed in with my hectic on-the-road-again schedule, I
did take some time out to give birth to two healthy, beautiful
children. In the case of Drew, though—my second born—the

62

fact that he came forth healthy and whole was nothing short of a miracle.

During my third month of pregnancy, it was discovered that some very toxic chemicals had leaked into the ashram water supply. I immediately went to the doctor for testing, and received a very gloomy prognosis. There was at least an 85% chance that my baby would be born severely brain damaged and deformed. As far as my physician was concerned, there was no option. A simple medical procedure, as he called it, would solve the problem.

What?? An abortion? **Murder** *my own child? What is this doctor, some kind of demon?* My tormented soul protested as I sat dumbfounded, listening to his recommendations.

Dr. Xavier decided to enlist support for his very ethical cause. In my follow-up visit, I was surrounded by six white-coats. Each one took a good bit of time explaining to me in serious medical terms what I was facing, bringing "a vegetable" into this world. Trying to speak my language, the oldest and most articulate of the doctors said that he did not believe it was God's will to have children born into this world with severe disabilities. The most loving and godly thing to do was to abort the fetus.

I went home bewildered. *What if I'm wrong? Isn't mercy killing an act of love? And what if the fetus is just a blob, and not really even a human being yet? Will I truly be able to love and raise this child if it doesn't look or act like a normal person? Why should I base my life on some stupid medical tests anyway?*

Reason told me clearly to have an abortion. My heart told me clearly to pray for a miracle. For the next six months I cried and prayed almost non-stop: "God, make my baby normal! Give me a healthy, beautiful child. Let this child be a joy and inspiration to his father and to the guru. Don't let there be anything wrong with this baby. God, Please!!!"

Exactly nine months and one day from the date of conception, a perfectly formed, adorable 7 lb. baby boy was born to me and Rembrandt. The good Lord was blessing me for turning to Him and keeping His commands, even though I was still confused about who He was.

Certainly, I was deeply grateful for the miracle of having a second son. But that thankfulness didn't change the fact that I just didn't have the heart or the spirit to stay home and nurture him myself. Besides that, my skills and chutzpah out on the mission field were very much in demand. So, with the help of the other ashram mothers, I was able to continue my traveling lifestyle and also keep my family life minimally intact. When I arrived home from my "mission for God" trips, my sons had already been potty trained and educated. However, they weren't quite sure which woman to call "Mom."

My perpetual absence from the ashram also affected Rembrandt. He had no one to bring meals to his art studio, to wash and fold his laundry, or to critique his color schemes and painting compositions. Although my husband really didn't want me to be singularly devoted to him, and he was happy that I was serving the guru in such an important way out on the mission field, there was a gaping hole in our relationship. A simple solution came to my mind—a second wife for Rembrandt.

Polygamy was indeed part of the Vedic culture, and as long as all parties were agreeable, the arrangement was considered a blessing. At first, I thought this was one of those "blessing" situations. Sita, a friend of mine, was eager to be married. I knew that Rembrandt would benefit from having a woman by his side on a day-to-day basis. My children longed for a stay-at-home mom to nurture and care for them, and Sita loved children. I was fired up to travel and preach. Win/win/win was all I could see as I enlisted my friend and my husband to share my vision of extended family.

But three weeks into the "blessing," I returned home from my purposeful travels only to find that Rembrandt and Sita had become very fond of one another. In fact, witnessing a joyful sparkle in both of their eyes, it became immediately clear to me that if their relationship culminated in marriage, I was going to be *the least favorite wife*, something I had neglected to consider upfront. This situation definitely needed to be nipped in the bud. Theory was one thing; emotional reality was another.

Fortunately, one disgruntled person in the threesome was enough to call the whole arrangement off, so it didn't take a whole lot of drama to redirect Sita's attentions away from Rembrandt, and Rembrandt's attentions back to his canvas and paints. (Shortly after this change of events, Sita left the ashram permanently, and became a born-again Christian). I returned to the streets with new fervor.

After quite a while, however, my super, high-functioning, itinerant lifestyle and questionable values definitely took their toll on me. I found myself plagued with nightmares, frequently dreaming that my children were lost and lonely. I could hear them crying out for me in the darkest nights. My heart was broken, but the strong beliefs that I held kept me from taking any emotions too seriously. *They're not really your children. These boys belong to God. He is caring for them through other surrogate mothers. There's no harm. They'll be strong.*

I also had disturbing dreams that I was being chased down by cops. My soul was not at rest with our fund-raising program. Legally, we were aboveboard, keeping between 30% and 50% of our collections for administrative and personal expenses. This percentage was minimal compared to the well-known national charity organizations that were keeping 60%-90% for the same purposes. Still, I felt compromised ethically and spiritually. The legalese mumbo jumbo that called me a "volunteer," even though I was pocketing a significant portion of the collections, wasn't sufficient to stave off my stress.

Finally, the issues of integrity within me could no longer be contained.

One day out on the fundraising field, I approached a very nice man with my usual bubbly presentation. He asked some sincere questions, wanting to make sure that his entire donation was truly going to help the needy. I froze. I was unable to respond. Tears began to pour down my cheeks.

I had presented this same appeal to people on the streets day after day, year after year, but this time I found myself singing a very strange sounding swan song. "You know what?" I said to the man in a sobbing voice, "I bet you have worthwhile charities at your church or in your office that you could give to. Why don't you just do that!" When I got home, I threw away all my fundraising paraphernalia. I was done. The Lord was at work in my heart.

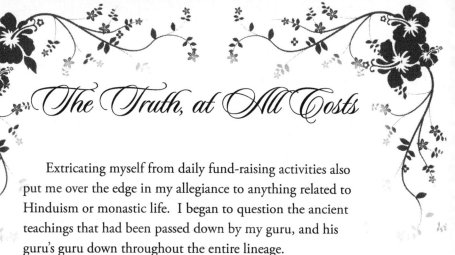

The Truth, at All Costs

Extricating myself from daily fund-raising activities also put me over the edge in my allegiance to anything related to Hinduism or monastic life. I began to question the ancient teachings that had been passed down by my guru, and his guru's guru down throughout the entire lineage.

For the next two years I investigated and scrutinized whatever I could get my hands on that had been written or spoken by my spiritual master. There were voluminous archives of books, letters and talks to which I had access. So I dove in deeply, looking for inconsistencies or any other signs that would discount the Vedas as the ultimate scriptures for me to base my life on. My search was relentless. I had to know the truth, whatever the cost.

The more I researched, the more I was faced with the soul-wrenching reality that what I had poured my entire adult life into was not what my heart was really hungering for. Certainly, the Hindu philosophical teachings and spiritual doctrines sounded true. I would read and memorize Sanskrit verses from the Bhagavad Gita that taught me to sow to the spirit, not to the flesh, and to separate myself from the world-ly patterns in order to cultivate noble virtues and devotional service. All this was wonderful daily spiritual food for my soul.

But something was wrong. Right from day one at the monastery, the representation of the supreme deity had caused me to stumble. I just was never able to accept that Krishna, a beautiful blue cowherd boy who plays the flute, is God. Every time I read about his "transcendental pastimes" of lifting Govardhana Hill with one finger, dancing with 108 cowherd girls simultaneously, and fighting off demons whose descriptions defied my wildest imagination, I would shake my head in concerned disbelief. These events seemed like fantastic fables and outrageous fairy tales, not absolute truth.

If Krishna is truly God, why isn't my heart stirred by revelations about him? How come every time I get around devotees who are relishing the recounting of Krishna's pastimes, I feel sick to my stomach and remove myself mentally, and whenever possible, physically? And why was it that other devotees were visited by Krishna and the guru in dreams, but I never was?

No matter how much I wanted to fully accept Krishna as the Supreme Personality of Godhead, it just wasn't happening. My heart was not being penetrated, and although I went through all the motions of worshipping the Krishna deity in the temple, hoping that my surrender and obedience would eventually transform into love, it never did.

I had chalked up my lack of acceptance and belief to being an immature, spiritual novice with a rebellious spirit. But month after month and year after year of serving as a stalwart disciple had not brought me to the conclusion I was seeking. If Krishna was the God of love, and the guru was God's messenger of love, it was only logical that twenty years of dedication to Krishna and the guru would have brought a great deal of love into my heart. That certainly was not the case. In fact, my heart felt cold and hard. There was no lack of spiritual exhilaration or zeal in my devotional life, but I was very far away from experiencing a sweet, warm, nurturing love.

As I continued to examine myself deeply, it became

excruciatingly clear to me that my monastic life was not built on the right foundation. I was trying to erect a fail-safe way of perfecting this lifetime, and securing my eternal destiny, in vain. All the worship, study of holy books, and selfless service in the world wasn't giving me true love or peace for my soul. I was a pathetic example of someone who had done all the right things, but had missed the boat.

Years later I was confronted with the perfect Biblical passage describing this dilemma: "*Though I speak with the tongues of men and of angels, but have not love, I have become sounding brass or a clanging cymbal. And though I have the gift of prophecy, and understand all mysteries and all knowledge, and though I have all faith, so that I could remove mountains, but have not love, I am nothing. And though I bestow all my goods to feed the poor, and though I give my body to be burned, but have not love, it profits me nothing*" (1 Corinthians 13:1-3). My highly cultivated and refined spirituality was meaningless with zero love attached to it. In my heart I felt completely bereft. What a disastrous, tragic corner I had painted myself into!

With these devastating realizations that I was going to have to break my sacred vows and find answers to life's deepest questions elsewhere, a dark night of the soul enveloped me that was blacker and more hopeless than anything I could ever have imagined.

As every part of me became unraveled, Rembrandt had his own revelations about changes that needed to happen in his personal life. We exited the ashram together, and on the heels of that departure, my husband decided to go his own separate way. Since Rembrandt had never really wanted to be married in the first place, but was simply following the guru's instructions for his life, and also because our marriage had been arranged and was not based on romantic love, Rembrandt felt trapped. I was willing to make any changes in myself or in our relationship that would be pleasing to him, but my supplications were to no avail.

Finally my soon-to-be ex-husband put it this way so I would understand: "Even if you dyed your hair purple, I still wouldn't want to stay married. There is nothing you can do." I got the message.

My already crumbled world completely caved in. The time I had spent in India learning how to make my husband my lord and master had worked against me. I had become very dependent on Rembrandt, and now he was leaving. I was totally crushed. There was absolutely no hope for me, a seriously distraught, spiritually confused, dysfunctional mother, with two fatherless children ... and no God.

I wept and wept and wept and wept and wept for months and months on end, to such a radical extreme that I had to have surgery on the unsightly, swollen areas around my eyes to calm them down and smooth them out. Finally, with nowhere to turn for comfort or strength, and unable to function beyond the daily survival necessities, I ended up sending my two boys to live with a friend. It was at this lowest of low points that I climbed into the waterless bathtub of my lonely, stark apartment prepared to take my own life, as I described at the beginning of this book. From there, it was a slow, arduous, excruciatingly painful, one-baby-step-at- a-time, climb upward.

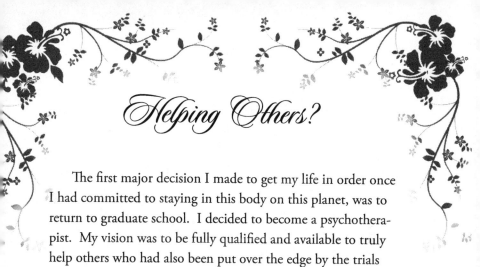

Helping Others?

The first major decision I made to get my life in order once I had committed to staying in this body on this planet, was to return to graduate school. I decided to become a psychotherapist. My vision was to be fully qualified and available to truly help others who had also been put over the edge by the trials and tribulations of life.

The more I learned about the teachings of Sigmund Freud, Carl Jung, Fritz Perls and the like, however, the farther away I felt that I was getting from the heart of true healing. When I was face-to-face with people who were hurting deeply, instead of empathizing lovingly with them, I would apply all the textbook principles I knew and analyze their psyches. Truthfully, this was not how I wanted to relate to people and their pain.

Keeping my clients at a professional distance so that I could maintain an ivory tower status felt hypocritical. On top of that, charging fees just added insult to injury. What I truly yearned for (though at the time I didn't know it) is highlighted in a powerful Biblical verse: "*Rejoice with those who rejoice, and weep with those who weep*" (Romans 12:15). My heart and soul wanted to be transparent and caring enough to share the burdens of those who were entrusting me with their sorrows.

I decided to drop out of the Masters program in psychology in which I was enrolled. In its place, I studied clinical hypnotherapy, which equipped me to assist people in breaking addictions and changing deep-seated patterns. When I hung out my first shingle in Tiburon, a very affluent town in the San Francisco bay area, some of the clients who found their way to my office were quite prominent, both in the community, and in the world. I felt privileged to be in a position to work with people of influence who had finally become broken enough to seek outside help.

Not all of my clients benefited from the clinical hypnotherapy sessions, however. In order to gain perspective on how to deal with those who didn't heal, despite what I considered to be proper assessment and treatment, I spoke to a friend who was an allopathic family doctor. Basically, he said that 1/3 of his patients would get well even without his help; 1/3 didn't respond to his treatments no matter what he did; and 1/3 actually benefitted from his care and got cured. It was for that 1/3 of the patients who healed in response to his doctoring that he continued to be a physician. These statistics were not very encouraging to me. I was hoping to be reassured that I had the power to help people out of their suffering. I was putting myself out as a "healer." I was discovering that title simply wasn't true.

Some very hard lessons came my way during the 15 years that I maintained a clinical hypnotherapy practice. Three of my clients ended up taking their own lives. Such tragedies forced me to reevaluate what I was really offering these people. They were placing their psyches and their inner lives under my care. *Was I really qualified to handle people's problems at such a core level? Was I playing God?*

The first disaster happened to a very striking, vivacious New Age dancer. She was going from man to man, to man, to man, falling in and out of love. Finally she gave up looking for fulfillment in all the wrong places and slit her wrists. My moralistic counsel and meditation techniques had no power to save her from destruction. After much soul-searching, I had to admit that I was about as lost as she was.

The second tragedy was reported to me via a phone call from a deputy sheriff in the mid-west. A young woman, who was one of my long-distance clients, was found dead in her home. By her side was a letter I had written to her with encouraging words and strong recommendations of daily spiritual disciplines that I believed would help her out of her funk if she adopted them. Apparently, I was wrong—dead wrong.

A final wake-up call that catapulted me out of my quasi-professional therapy practice took place in a jewelry store. The jeweler was intently listening to the news on his radio as I approached an illuminated showcase. Picking out a very beautiful ruby ring to present to me for my inspection, but still seeming distracted and saddened by the news report, he leaned forward and almost gasped for breath as he transferred the ring into my hand. "Jerry Garcia is dead. The Grateful Dead era is over. How is this possible? Jerry is our hero!" This hit me hard. Jerry had been my client. I was shocked; shaken to the core. *Why didn't Jerry listen to me? I told him he wasn't ready to go back on tour! Why didn't I insist that he cancel his concerts?*

Then I got it. What I was offering my clients was not only useless, but in some cases, irrevocably harmful. This was a situation of the blind leading the blind. Some of those who were following my misguided leadership ended up in a dark pit, never to come out. By God's grace only, I somehow did come out of the pit, many years later.

Miracle in Divorce Court

The road to hell is paved with good intentions kept running through my brain, as I tried to resolve what was going on with such disastrous results in my therapy practice. Without clear knowledge of absolute truth, it certainly was possible to be stuck on a path of darkness, thinking that because my heart was in the right place, that I was on a path of light. But even my best desires for the healing of others were leading some of my clients into darkness and death. I surely did not know as much as I thought I did.

My own inner turmoil that I was trying to sublimate by ministering to others rather than facing myself head-on finally demanded that I do something radical. The last time I had come to this place of deep despair, I took matters into my own hands. I was planning to kill myself. But this time I made up my mind that I was going to confront God (whoever He was) and demand some immediate action on His part. After all, if He was omnipotent and omniscient, and things weren't going well for me, it was up to Him to fix the situation.

I had seen a picture of the Wailing Wall in Israel, and filed it away in my consciousness as a last resort kind of place. Since I wasn't about to head off to the Holy Land to talk to God, but I was at the end of my rope, I decided to face a wall in my sweet little cottage in the Aptos woods in California, and completely let loose. At this point I was absolutely furious with God, and had no interest in being nicey-nice in my communications.

You horrible God! How dare You treat Your daughter like this. You expect worship and service, and all You give back is pure hell. I'm done, do You hear me? DONE!

Fortunately, none of my neighbors were home, or I am quite certain they would have thought I was being murdered. My hysterical screaming was that intense.

Of all the unreconciled issues I had with God—and there were many—the first and foremost was that I still was not united with my soul mate. I assumed that my two marital fiascos had been the result of lack of discernment and immaturity on my part, and lack of protection and care on God's part. This time, I was going to be more proactive.

When I calmed down enough to think clearly, I wrote down a list of 52 qualities and character traits that described Mr. Right, according to my very specific standards. I read this list out loud to my personal wailing wall, as if the wall were the recipient of divine petitions. Two days later, I met Leonard. This hardly seemed like a coincidence.

As it turned out, my friends who introduced me to Leonard, were right on the money about the two of us being extremely compatible. On the second day of our meeting, we sat down together with my "ideal mate" list and checked off 48 of the 52 qualities I had written down. Leonard was very, very close to what I was looking for. Serendipitously, I was almost exactly what he was looking for. A "marriage made in heaven" was in the making.

Three years later we tied the knot. Our honeymoon period lasted for an absolutely amazing ten days. Then the dirt hit the fan. It seemed that I had asked God for *my* vision of the perfect man for me, not *His*. My new husband and I were not as well suited to each other as we had thought. What I imagined would make me happy, was actually making me desperately miserable. Perhaps to teach me to rely on Him, rather than championing my own ideas in my petitions, what I received in response to my reckless pleas for Mr. Right was Mr. Always Right.

Leonard was an outstandingly successful business man and a bottom line kind of guy. After seven years of a rocky relationship with me, he realized that this particular "business of love" just wasn't going in an upward direction. So, he ordered me to divorce court and brought out the big guns for a major battle. When you are dealing with seven figure settlements, you need to be on your toes. Just about anything can happen.

The judge entered the courtroom and called the court to order. Immediately, a supernatural occurrence took place. As the gavel hit the judge's desk, the words, *"Settle with your brother on the way to court"* resounded in my left ear. No one was sitting to my left. My attorney, sitting to my right, sensed that I was becoming undone. She leaned over and asked me if I was ready to proceed. My mind and heart were going wild.

Get me out of here now! I'm not going through with this!! I'm not going to fight for money. There's something wrong with this whole thing! I used to be in love with that man. This can't possibly be God's way to resolve misunderstandings!

What was taking place inside me was completely transcendental. I was not recalling the admonition of the Master in Luke 12:58: *"When you go with your adversary to the magistrate, make every effort along the way to settle with him…"* That teaching was unfamiliar to me at that time in my life. But, somehow, by grace alone, I knew that it was Jesus Christ who was directing me to withdraw immediately from this hostile situation.

What ensued was a classic spiritual struggle. The Lord had

spoken. His words were so weighty that they stopped me in my tracks. This divine message stood up firmly against the fast-talking, urgent counseling of my attorney: "You're stressed out and can't think straight. You will regret this crazy decision for the rest of your life. We have the law completely on our side. You can set yourself up *very* comfortably for life now. You'll never have to worry about money again.. You can't change horses in mid-stream! Don't listen to your mind!!"

It was not my mind I was listening to. It was Yeshua, the deliverer of my soul. I was immovable. I refused to continue with the proceedings.

Although at that time I didn't know who Jesus really was, I could not discount His spiritual counsel. I was compelled from within my heart to follow. I asked my lawyer to get me just enough money to live on very modestly for one year, as I got my life together. Leonard could keep all the fat bank accounts and costly possessions. What I was asking for was so ridiculously minimal that there was no contest at all. I imagine that this was the quickest divorce settlement in history. Ten minutes later, the papers were signed. The divorce was finalized. I was free, and easy, and poor, by the world's standards.

Soul-Stirring Events

When I look back to that miraculous time in divorce court, when the Lord made Himself known to me in an irresistible manner, I wonder if I had been prepared for that amazing revelation by four very significant events that had taken place during the seven-year period when Leonard and I were together.

The first occurrence happened in a picture perfect, rose-colored church. The service was led by a gorgeous looking female minister, who began the sermon reading from the Bible some heart-piercing words that were brand new to me:

"Come to Me, all you who labor and are heavy laden, and I will give you rest. Take My yoke upon you, and learn from Me, for I am gentle and lowly in heart, and you will find rest for your souls. For My yoke is easy and My burden is light" (Matthew 11:28-30).

I had never heard such loving, beautiful, comforting words. I was touched down to the core of my being. Tears poured down my cheeks, my heart throbbed, and the remainder of the service got lost in my muffled weeping. I left the church that Sunday bewildered, but intrigued, by what had taken place.

I returned to the rose-colored church the next week, hoping for another profound experience, but this time I became aware that the focus of the church's mission was not Jesus Himself, but self-empowerment. This was not a traditional Christian fellowship, but a New Age congregation. All the beautiful people, exquisite clothing, uplifting music, and cushy chairs certainly had some appeal—especially being sprinkled with a few Bible verses here and there. But I wasn't looking for a more attractive life here on earth. I was looking for eternal rest for my wrenched and weary soul.

The next church I decided to check out was a huge stretch for me. I didn't know what the label "fundamentalist Christian" meant, but I knew that I felt completely out of place around people who called themselves fundamentalist Christians. In spite of this, I went alone to a fairly large fundamentalist Christian church and sat right up front, so if there was an anointing taking place at the pulpit, it would pour out on me. Looking around at the six hundred or so congregants, I couldn't find one person who looked like my type. Talk about being a fish out of water!

I was just about ready to bolt for the exit door when the praise and worship music began. Immediately, the whole atmosphere was transformed. I felt strangely and completely at home. Joy welled up in my heart. Here I was, singing beautiful love songs to a God these people seemed to know very intimately. *How was this possible?* I felt more at home and more at peace being in a room full of peculiar-looking strangers than I did anywhere else. What was going on?

As the service came to an end, the pastor asked the praise and worship team to continue the music as an anointing bath for those who wanted to stay in the sanctuary and have a quiet time with the Lord. I found a place on the floor near a beautiful Mexican-looking young man who was crying deeply and praying out loud with a sweet accent.

Somehow, I didn't feel that I was eavesdropping as I listened intently to this young man's magnificent outpourings. "Jesus, sweet gentle Jesus, Lord of my soul. I love you with all my heart. Thank you, thank you. Thank you for dying on the cross and delivering me from my dark, useless life. Thank you for redeeming me. Please, Lord Jesus, what are my next steps in serving you? I live only to do your will. Guide me Lord, and please have mercy on my friend, Jake." I had never witnessed anything like this. What this young man had, an intimate, personal, grateful, humble relationship with God, I craved. Finally, *this was it*!

Everything I had been seeking through all my radical, intense, excruciatingly painful, soul-wrenching, relentless pursuits was right here before my eyes, and within my hearing range. This was true love. Here was a humble soul with a contrite spirit, who had fully received the free gift of the new covenant of grace. I wanted to stay right where I was on that floor, at the foot of the cross, near that beautiful lover of Christ for all eternity.

Witnessing a broken saint in the presence of his Beloved left an indelible impression on my innermost being. Although I had certainly heard the gospel message preached many times at the pulpit and on the streets, this was the first time I ever really understood it.

After this very profound experience, I was yearning to return to that fellowship, but because all my family and friends were so completely against that type of Christian church, I decided I wasn't ready to leap out completely on my own. Instead, I continued on with my eclectic spiritual practices. God continued to pursue me. Knowing what a hard nut I was to crack, He used ingenious methods to woo me closer.

The next amazing occurrence happened at a New Age retreat center where I was staying for a couple of weeks. I was in an unusually cold meeting room with thirty other retreat participants who were beginning to complain about the temperature. The leader then entered the room and singled me out to find out what the problem was.

"Do you have your finger on the pulse of this room?" Arthur asked me, almost metaphysically. My response came flying out of my mouth quite unconsciously: "Many are cold; a few are frozen." Some of the retreat participants burst out laughing hysterically. I had to agree that my words sounded stilted and odd, but there seemed to be a private joke that I wasn't getting. Finally, someone clued me in. He quoted Matthew 22:14 from the New Testament: *"For many are called, but few are chosen."*

What a divine set-up! These words resonated profoundly in my soul. For the remainder of the retreat, my mind was preoccupied. I could hardly wait to get somewhere to investigate the Biblical context and meaning of these intriguing words. The Lord was drawing me closer in fascinating and mysterious ways. He seemed to be using a backdoor approach, because honestly, I was the type who would try to jump the fence rather than enter the sheepfold through the narrow gate.

Sometime after returning home from the retreat, another event took place that I believe helped to prepare me for the miracle that happened in divorce court, when Jesus spoke to me to withdraw from the legal contest.

Leonard and I were moving out of our house, and I had hired some people who advertised themselves as "moving angels" to come and do a final deep cleaning. When the "angels" arrived, I discovered that it was a family of four, very radiant, joyful Christians. They sang hymns as they worked, touched all my possessions with deep love, and prayed over every corner of the house. My home felt like a beautiful, Spirit-filled church by the time they were finished.

These people certainly were the Lord's ambassadors, and because they sensed that I was open to hearing what they had to say, they explained their ministry to me. They were not simply cleaning houses; they were bringing the light, the peace, and the joy of the Lord Jesus Christ wherever they went. Although I didn't have the Biblical terminology to describe what I experienced in their presence, I just knew that these family members were walking their talk. They carried God's love and truth in their hearts, mouths, and hands. Using rags and household cleaners, they were blessing all my possessions, and praying that everything in my life would be redeemed for the Lord's service. I found myself praying the same prayer.

One of Them

With very little money in my pocket after my divorce from Leonard and lots of time on my hands, I decided to get a job selling art in a small gallery in downtown Kona, on the Big Island of Hawaii. I was not aware that the art gallery was the mission field of a popular Christian painter. I also had no idea that my boss was a believer in Jesus Christ, and that she had an evangelical spirit.

At the beginning of my sales training, I found myself struggling with mixed feelings. I loved the fact that the small staff came together and began each work day with prayer, but I resented the fact that the way I prayed was not acceptable to my boss. What was wrong with praying to Mother Mary and the angels, along with God Himself? Why did I need to pray in Jesus' name? Why couldn't I quote from *The Aquarian Gospel of Jesus the Christ* and *A Course in Miracles*, both of which were purported to be the direct teachings of Jesus Christ? After all, the others who prayed were quoting from the Bible. What did the gallery staff mean when they said I didn't know the REAL Jesus?

Not much was penetrating or illuminating. I just knew I didn't fit into what seemed to be a very elitist, intolerant Christian world. I couldn't even figure out why I was hired to work there if I wasn't "one of them." Little did I know that I was soon to become "one of them," and that my Lord was pursuing me and drawing me closer.

Several months after working at the art gallery, I found that my broken heart was not mending very well. I would frequently pass Leonard on the road of the small town in which we lived just south of Kona. Each time I saw him driving around with a different woman in "our" sporty BMW convertible, I would end up crying bitterly. My wounds were too raw to live in such close quarters to my ex. So I decided to quit my job and move back to California, where I had a large community of supportive friends.

A Highly Suspect Prophet

Landing back in California was both shocking and overwhelming for me. I had become accustomed to the Hawaiian lifestyle and its relaxed pace, and my nervous system felt traumatized by the busier, denser environment of the mainland. Witnessing my discomfort, a friend invited me to a gathering of a burgeoning spiritual group. "You'll find refuge and healing sitting under the teachings of this messenger from God," Mark told me very compassionately. I was willing to try just about anything at this point.

Mark and I arrived on time for the event, but the large hotel conference room was already filled to capacity. There was standing room only, and lines out the door. Hundreds of people were there talking about the guru celebrity who would soon be speaking. Most of those in attendance were her devoted disciples. I felt excited at the prospect of coming face-to-face with someone who was reputed to have been sent directly from God to bring healing to the planet. Certainly, she would be able to help save me from all my despair and confusion!

The master entered, sat down, and began to teach. From where I was standing, I was unable to hear her at all and could only get occasional glimpses of what she looked like. Something struck me as hauntingly familiar, though. Observing the crowd hanging on the speaker's every word, I decided to squeeze my way up towards front center so I could figure out what was going on. The voice and the person matched up. I broke out in a curious smile. The well-beloved master was Chelsea, my former ashram friend and fund-raising partner!

Chelsea had a way about her that was quite irresistible when she was out in the field collecting donations from total strangers, and that same spiritual magnetism was clearly running the show here with her disciples. When my old ashram "god-sister" (as we called one another) personally invited me to join her tightly knit spiritual community, I gladly accepted the offer.

There were several thousands of followers of Chelsea's teachings worldwide who lived in very lovely, impeccably-cared-for, communal houses. The household I became an integral part of was at the farthest end of the wonderful town of Poway in Southern California, where the sound of coyotes was about the only distraction we had. Seven of us shared food, rent, and some simple possessions, very much like the Acts 2:44-45 model of the early Christian church body: *"Now all who believed were together, and had all things in common, and sold their possessions and goods, and divided them among all, as anyone had need."* The sharing made sense. That was not the problem. The problem was what we believed.

Chelsea had read the New Testament, and it was not unlike her to take certain Biblical principles out of context and apply them to situations that resembled the true Christian walk, but did not have the purity or the power of God to back them up. This communal lifestyle was one of those questionable situations.

Even so, the one-body, one-mind, one-heart aspect of this organization did appeal to me, and in my way of thinking, stuff was just stuff. There was no mine and yours. Everything belonged to God, and things could be moved around and shared as needed. I was very comfortable with the idea of owning nothing.

But where I kept hitting a wall was with the idea of a *new revelation* as the foundation of this spiritual group. Although Chelsea drew from the teachings of Jesus Christ, she did not present the Scripture, or encourage us to read the Bible directly. There was no meat to chew on, only the guidance of the "enlightened teacher" in our midst who was claiming to be an apostle of truth directly from the Creator.

I wrestled with serious doubts as to whether what sounded like a vastly exaggerated claim could actually be true, but I was willing to give it my best shot.

By this time I had become aware that even Jesus was not accepted in his home town; that prophets don't receive honor among their own people. So, if I was having a hard time accepting that my old friend, Chelsea was an ambassador from God who was sent to help deliver mankind, that doubting made perfect sense spiritually. There were several thousand other people who didn't have the background connection I had with Chelsea who easily accepted her authenticity.

After a number of very difficult, intense years as a member of Chelsea's unorthodox church, I could no longer override the deep concerns that plagued my heart and soul. I had been given special privileges and a tremendous amount of love and support as one of the master's personal friends, which made my involvement in the community quite enjoyable. However, when push came to shove, I wasn't really sure that I had made any significant progress on the spiritual path, immersing myself in Chelsea's home-grown and radically unpredictable teachings about God.

The turning point for me was when I received a phone call

from one of the main church leaders, a young man who happened to be an heir to a mega-Fortune 500 company. He told me very bluntly that he wanted to move into the very beautiful house that I was sharing with several other devotees, and that I was to move out right away—that day, in fact. My mind raced through all the spiritual teachings that I had been studying, but in spite of my meditations on the true meaning of humility, selflessness, sacrifice, and surrender, I couldn't come up with any noble thoughts that would quell my anger. I was furious. Livid, in fact. *Who did this guy think he was? And, was Chelsea behind this?*

That was it. It was over for me. There had been one weird thing after another happening in the name of God in this organization for years. One couple was told by Chelsea on their wedding night that they had misinterpreted the signs that the Lord had sent them, and in truth, they were not supposed to be together. Their marriage was terminated before it even began. Other people were instructed randomly to quit their jobs, move here and there, watch TV, don't watch TV, wear this, don't wear that, etc., all based on the supposed promptings from God Himself. Compared to what some of the other devotees were dealing with, the sudden eviction from my house wasn't even that significant, but it did put me over the edge. I decided that if this church was in fact God's family, I would prefer to be an orphan.

Drawn to Bible College

Pushed again to the breaking point, I signed a document of apostasy proclaiming that I had turned my back on the "divine dispensation" that was coming through Chelsea's group and was willing to accept the "eternal consequences."

The next day, I decided to return to my old stomping grounds where I had often gone for refreshment and restoration—Murrieta Hot Springs, in Southern California. As I approached the front gate, I knew immediately that something was drastically different. The once quiet and meditative retreat center had been transformed into a quickened, white-hot, spiritual beehive. Seven hundred bright-eyed Christian students from all over the world were preparing for the commencement of Calvary Chapel Bible College, which was to begin in three days.

Although there was nothing about the new environment or the people that called to me at all, there was a burning compulsion in my heart to jump in, head first. The minimal exposure I had already experienced with the Bible had been sufficient to whet my appetite for more intense study and understanding.

Compared to other spiritual texts, the Word of God stood out as being *the only book* that actually stirred up my heart and alchemized my very nature as I read it. Other religious teachings were very similar to Biblical precepts. But what they didn't have was the "God-breathed" transforming power to perform spiritual surgery on my life. The difference was very apparent to me, since

I was so deeply in need of change from the inside out.

Excited about the prospect of plugging in to an actual institute of higher learning that could support me in my relentless quest for truth, I went to the college office and was given a tour of the classrooms and dorm facilities. The two people who showed me around the campus were incredulous as I sincerely tried to make the logistics work. "Are you kidding, lady?" their countenances were clearly saying. "You're not even a Christian, you're 54 years old, and you're going to put all your possessions in storage and in three days, move into a dorm with a bunch of 20-year-olds so you can study the Bible? *What* are you thinking??"

My personal hosts finally derailed me to the bookstore where my spirit went absolutely wild. I began to salivate as I looked around. I had no idea that there was a whole world of Christian literature that taught the deep things of God. With only a half hour to explore all of this spiritual wealth before the book store closed, I prayed to be guided to the right book to begin my studies, even before the classes began.

I walked directly to one shelf and pulled out a small, ordinary looking, hardbound book. It was entitled *At the Master's Feet*, and was a daily devotional with selections from the best of Charles Spurgeon. Aside from Billy Graham, I had never heard of any Christian teachers or authors. For all I knew, Spurgeon was some obscure spiritual novice who barely had anything to say worth listening to.

By the time I had purchased the little book and left the store, however, I had perused enough of the pages to realize that what I held in my hands was written by *the* silver-tongued preacher. What I didn't know was that Charles H. Spurgeon was to become my first absent-in-the-body spiritual father and discipler several years later.

Driving away from Murrieta, I noticed that something wasn't clicking. As much as I wanted to devote myself to a serious investigation of Christianity, this somehow didn't feel like the right time or the right place to do that. Instead, I chose to head up north to Harbin Hot Springs, a large international retreat center just outside the beautiful Napa Valley.

Crying in the car all the way from Southern California to Northern California, I desperately hoped and prayed that the next chapter of my life would give me the answers to my soul's urgent questions.

Being a pilgrim, with a light touch on the world, did have its advantages; I could just pick up and go without looking back. But, what I was going *to* was uncertain. *More heartache? More disappointment? More confusion? More torture for my soul? Would God ever reveal Himself to me in a way that I could find peace and rest?*

The Channeling Detour

When I pulled up to the entrance at Harbin Hot Springs, something instantly relaxed in my nervous system. Harbin was the kind of place where it was more than okay to feel lost and disillusioned. The lovely, deer-laden grounds were filled with people from all over the world who were trying to figure out why their lives weren't working the way they wanted them to. I fit right in to this tentative human landscape, since at that point in my misguided pilgrimage, I no longer trusted myself to make wise, or even sane, decisions.

For the first three months of my stay, I removed myself from all social interactions by shaving my head, maintaining silence, and soaking in hot mineral baths, except for a few hours a day when I performed housekeeping activities in exchange for room and board at the retreat center. Withdrawn from the Harbingers (as the residents were called), the world and its accoutrements, I begged God quietly but deeply, to help me. Once again, I was at my wits end. I was desperate.

As I took inventory of my sorrowful life, I recognized that my relentless journey up until that point had been what the Indian mystics call *neti neti*; not this, not that. Nothing in my life seemed to be what my soul was ultimately longing for. I had been born and raised Jewish. It was not this. I had been a high school English teacher. It was not that. I had spent years high on psychedelics. It was not this. I had lived in a Hindu monastery for twenty years. It was not that. I had been the wife of a multi-millionaire. It was not this. I had walked out on a huge divorce settlement. It was not that. I had led women's empowerment groups, *A Course in Miracles* studies, relationship seminars, and rebirthing workshops in New Age spiritual communities. It was not this. I had been a counselor and a clinical therapist. It was not that.

The process of elimination path to finding the truth clearly wasn't the way. I still didn't know who I was, who God was, or what the purpose of life was. It hit me that I didn't really feel any better off than I did thirty years earlier, when I first embarked upon my focused spiritual quest. *Had I been on an arduous, but useless, journey? Where were the fruits of all my endeavors?*

By the end of my three-month silent period of prayer and contemplation, my hair was growing back a little. Even though I looked pretty freaky with tiny little ringlets all over my head, I felt ready to be out in a public setting. I decided to attend a musical event in the main hall of the retreat center.

At the conclusion of the concert, a man whom I had never seen before approached me and challenged me with an off-the-wall remark. "You channel Mother Mary, don't you?" he ventured. I responded by saying that I did not do any channeling, but that if he was looking for some personal counseling, I could offer him that. He took me up on my offer, and we did what I considered to be a standard talk therapy session. As our time together came to an end, the man handed me a $100 bill and said very nonchalantly, "That was Mother Mary!" I was astonished.

At that time in my life, I was not a big fan of channeling at all. I had been around quite a few channelers before, and frankly, I found them to be boring and highly suspect. Lots of ear-tickling love and light messages always came pouring forth from the mediums, making me wonder how much was truth, and how much was flattery. There was one channeler, however, who had published a number of best-selling self-help books whom I really did trust and respect. I decided to sign up for a weekend workshop that she and her husband were giving.

On the second day of the workshop, the New Age prophets, as they were generally considered to be by their followers, had an irreconcilable fight right in front of all their students. There were about 20 participants in the room, and one by one each one of us tried to help the teachers get through their stuff. But, nothing seemed to work. Apparently, the walls Shanti and her husband were hitting were impenetrable. Their deep relational issues had been long-standing. These well-known teachers were operating on the very popular New Age tenet that "you teach what you most need to learn," something that never really made sense to me. I was more of the conviction that you should only teach what you have mastered.

During an afternoon break, I found Shanti alone in a hot tub nestled in the garden outside our meeting room. I decided to join her and see if I could get her take on what was going on. "How is it possible that you can have so much spiritual knowledge, but you're not able to apply these principles effectively in your own marriage?" I asked quite innocently, hoping for some profound explanation. "My books are all channeled," Shanti replied with casual non-involvement. "They have absolutely nothing to do with me."

This response really got me thinking. *Was channeling simply a way of not taking personal responsibility? Was it a highfalutin, mystical-sounding cop-out? How could this particular author and workshop leader have risen to the top of the New Age if she,*

herself, wasn't getting healed? Where did the channeled informa-
tion come from, anyway, and did it truly have the power of God
behind it? I wanted to stay open to all possibilities—after all,
I knew that God had no limits—but, I also didn't want to be
misled ever again.

The channeling phenomenon did make an impression on
me, but I relegated it to a backseat place in my consciousness
for the next year and a half, or so. During that time I met
Justice, who was destined to become my husband and fellow
traveler on my radical and intense journey Home.

The Ultimate Matchmaker

When I first noticed Justice walking around the very serene, mountainous grounds of Harbin in Middletown, California, something struck me. There was an attractive aloofness to this man's spirit that complimented his classic good looks. The notebook and clipboard he was carrying only added to the compelling mystique that surrounded his being. I wanted to know who this blonde-haired athletic looking guy was.

I decided to ask one of the residents if she had a read on this man. I realized he could very well have been from Timbuktu, considering the fact that world travelers came and went from this hot springs community all the time.

"What?" Jessica looked at me quizzically, as I pointed to Justice who happened to be walking down the path nearby. "You mean the tennis guy? No way! You've got to be kidding. You're interested in the tennis guy? Good luck!!" she said mischievously as she disappeared down the dirt road to the Harbin restaurant. Jessica obviously knew something about Justice that she wasn't even considering sharing with me at this point.

A couple of days later, I stopped in to the health services office to make an appointment for a massage, and *there he was*, sitting behind the reception desk, running the place. As I made my way towards control central, Justice's basilisk blues took me in from head to toe. His curiously shy smile and outstandingly bright countenance indicated that I was in the right place at the right time, showing up in exactly the right way. I lost my composure.

"I bet you're from the San Diego area," I ventured, recognizing the outdoorsy, preppy look of the Southern California men.

"I am," he said, amazed at my perceptiveness.

"What part?"

"North County."

"North County?? You're from North County?" *This is getting weird.* "Do you happen to know Rembrandt?"

"Of course, I know Rembrandt. He was in my men's group. YOU are Rembrandt's ex-wife? I can't believe it! He told me you would be here. I've really been looking forward to meeting you! This is wonderful!"

What are the chances of this happening? Almost zero. This IS weird! God must be behind this whole thing!

Within a few weeks and in a very tender manner, Justice had invited me to be his healing partner. I didn't know what the function of a healing partner was. In fact, I had never heard of a healing partner before. But this invitation sure sounded like an exciting opportunity to participate in some kind of a deep spiritual relationship. And it was. Very quickly, Justice and I bared our souls to one another, and mutual feelings of love stirred in our hearts.

It didn't take long before this tennis guy was telling me that I was an amazing gift from God, and that he was very much in love with my consciousness. "Being with you is like being alone," Justice would frequently tell me, letting me know that he felt totally at home in my presence. In addition, he would look deeply and lovingly at me, cherishing every minute detail of my femininity, shake his head in joyful disbelief, and ponder out loud, "Where did you come from?" This was exactly the way I needed to be courted. My romantic inclinations were

97

way outside the standard Hollywood package. Somehow, this man spoke the language of my soul, and quickly found his way into my heart.

Justice and I soon discovered that we matched up like a well-fitting pair of favorite shoes. But we also recognized that despite the uncanny configuration of extremely compatible elements, we were still an odd couple, of sorts. Justice was an ex-jock. I was an ex-monk. Justice enjoyed unwinding in front of the TV at the end of the day. I hadn't owned or watched a TV in over 30 years. Justice earned his master's degree in leisure studies. I was a serious workaholic. He had been an unusually sexually active bachelor much of his adult life. I had maintained celibacy much of mine. We both were aware right from the beginning of our meeting, however, that something special was being orchestrated from on high.

The surety that God was behind our union prompted Justice and me to make a major change six months after we had come together as a couple. Filling up the front room of Justice's house with our joint possessions, and inviting all the Harbin residents to a free give-away, we joyfully let go of clothing, books, treasured gifts, and furniture. There was very little we wanted to hold on to. We had an intense love for each other, money in the bank, a very sturdy tent, and a mission—to discover why God had brought us together, and what we were supposed to do about it.

Hawaii seemed like the best place for us to relocate, so we flew to the Big Island, pitched our tent on a magnificent semi-private beach, built an outdoor kitchen out of rocks, driftwood, and tarps, and settled into the relaxing spirit of aloha. The amazing make-shift home that we put together, overlooking a sea turtle haven, was so nurturing and uplifting that we probably would still be living there … if it hadn't been for Pastor Billy.

Pastor Billy and his prominent Hawaiian family happened to own a lovely property that backed up to the same beach where we had set up camp. After a couple of months' grace period (by this time we had purchased a second large tent and were creating a very comfortable idyllic homestead), Pastor Billy decided to call the county authorities to remove us from the beach. We were given no warning at all that there was a problem with us living there.

When the county rangers showed up, it was very obvious what was going through their minds. All they could manage to say was "We're really sorry, guys. Just doing our job. This is really nice, what you've set up here. Let's see; two room-sized tents and a cooking area, that's about all you need, isn't it? We'd let you stay, but you know, Uncle Billy…" In Hawaii, especially on the Big Island, you don't mess around with Uncle *anyone*.

Once the authorities completed their task and left, we tracked down Pastor Billy. "Why didn't you come to us and tell us personally that you didn't want us staying here?" we asked, wondering how someone could care for an entire church flock but be clueless how to deal directly with his closest neighbor. "Can't you see that we're living a very peaceful, clean, beautiful life, and not bothering anyone? If anything, our presence here is a protection for your home." Pastor Billy broke down. Once he met us face to face and heard our story, he regretted how he had handled the situation.

"Come. Let us pray together," Pastor Billy spoke tear-fully as he encircled Justice and me with his ample Hawaiian arms, drawing us into a huddle: "Father God, we come before

You humbly today, seeking Your favor. I know that You have prepared the perfect home for this loving couple, and I ask that You please allow that home to find them, God. Bring it right to them, so they will know that You are watching over them and that You are their Provider. Thank You, Lord. I pray in the name of Jesus Christ. Amen."

By the time I had hugged Pastor Billy goodbye, I understood that this whole episode had been part of God's plan. No one had ever prayed for me quite like that before. This man of God had a good grasp on how the Lord of the universe operates. It was worth losing our little piece of paradise to be brought before the throne of grace in such an intimate, powerful way.

We found out later that Pastor Billy was somewhat of a legend on the Big Island of Hawaii. It really was a blessing to have him as a support person. The prayers Billy offered up for our perfect home to find us were answered within one week.

Responding to a request of a friend of a friend to call someone and say "Hi," the words of heaven came back to us over the phone. "You don't happen to be looking for a place to live, do you? I have a cottage for rent in the papaya fields that just became available. How's $300 a month?" Of course, it *was* the ideal place for us; an absolute Godsend, major fixer-upper with deeply hidden, but outstanding potential.

Several months later, after Justice and I were settled into our beautifully remodeled home, we showed up unexpectedly at Pastor Billy's church on the other side of the island for a Sunday service. When he spotted us, he shouted in joyful disbelief to his wife, "Honey. Look who's here!! I can't believe it. They forgave me! It's a miracle. They forgave me! Thank you, Lord."

The Christian dispensation was definitely seeping into

our lives in interesting ways. And so were other dispensations from the spiritual realms. We were open to all of it. In fact we were so open, that for a very long time, we didn't have a lot of discernment.

Remember that man who informed me that I had channeled Mother Mary for him and then handed me a $100 bill to let me know that the information that he had received was truly helpful? Well, that was the beginning of a five year spiritual phenomenon.

A familiar spirit in the likeness of Mother Mary started showing up in my meditations on a regular basis. I felt truly honored. This feminine presence appeared as an audible teacher and a comforting guide. The otherworldly voice, speaking through me in a semi-conscious state, gave counsel to seekers who were bringing their most sincere life questions before her.

Channeled messages were also delivered through me by automatic writing, and four years after our first encounters with "Mother Mary," Justice and I published a book containing spiritual guidelines for man/woman relationship. We were quite certain that this information had come directly from the mother of Jesus. It all seemed very godly and righteous. Our belief was that we had been chosen and blessed to deliver this very important information—a new revelation—to the planet.

There was a major problem, though. Like Shanti, the channeler I mentioned before, who was fighting irreconcilably with her husband at the relationship seminar they were teaching, Justice and I were not able to put the principles that had come forth from the presenting spirit "Mother Mary" into practice very well. Not only were we always falling short, but the teachings themselves became questionable in my mind and heart.

Could these channelings actually be from the spirit realm, but not directly from God, the Truth? Is it possible that things are not what they appear to be? I am being told by others who are present at the channelings that when I go into a trance and the familiar spirit in the likeness of Mother Mary comes upon me, I am enveloped in peace and light. Is this even true? I don't feel peaceful when I'm channeling. I feel hesitant and concerned. The spirit of fear isn't from God. Something must be wrong!

Whatever doubts I was having about the authenticity of the "divine" information that was being delivered and its source were escalated when I met Marion. Marion was an ex-trance channel, reborn in the Spirit of Christ. "What are you doing?!" Marion screamed at me pointedly when I shared what was going on in my life. You stop this channeling, *or else*!!"

Marion proceeded to confront me with serious accusations. According to her knowledgeable assessment, I was misrepresenting the truth and misleading people. Marion told me in no uncertain terms that if I didn't stop bringing forth messages from the so-called mother of Jesus Christ, she would personally do everything in her power to create trouble for me. The fire in her eyes convinced me that I was up against a very determined force.

I decided to take Marion's warnings to heart, not so much because I thought she was right, but because I didn't want to deal with the repercussions of her anger. Even though Justice and I had witnessed many people receiving benefit from the channeled information that we had disseminated, I no longer wanted the burden of delivering messages from *who-knows-where* on my shoulders. My channeling days were numbered. And as it turned out, so were my delightful, romantic honeymoon days with Justice.

Spiritual Deficiency

As C.S. Lewis put it in his book *A Severe Mercy*, when it comes to romantic relationships, "there is no eternal spring." In other words, sooner or later, both lovers will have to face the hard reality that the initial infatuation that brought them together so magically wears thin after a while. Both Justice and I certainly knew this to be a fact from past conjugal relationships, but our fresh, starry-eyed union tricked us into thinking that what we were experiencing together this time was completely different. Maybe an eternal spring wasn't the rule of romantic love, but what about an endless summer?

Because we were so convinced that God had joined us and had gifted us sumptuously with a blissful adoration of one another, Justice and I committed ourselves to doing anything and everything we could imagine to hold on to that ecstatic union. But the truth was, it just wasn't sustainable. We still found ourselves seriously disheartened as time went on.

Darkness entered my marriage. I found myself on an emotional roller coaster. A fading love affair and menopausal symptoms are not the greatest combination for optimum health and well-being, and in my case, my physical body was seriously affected by my spun out inner world.

Being sick soon became a way of life for me, as it had several times in the past when my emotions had become disturbed and unstable. The medical doctors provided diagnoses and medicines, but I wasn't interested in just curing the symptoms of dis-ease that were manifesting in the flesh. I knew deep inside myself that if I really wanted to get well through and through, I would have to get to the root of the problem. Physical sickness was the outward symptom of an inward condition. I was heart sick and soul sick.

Justice and I had heard about a "miracle man" in Brazil, John of God, who supposedly had cured millions of people of all kinds of serious illnesses. People were flocking from all over the world to come to his *casa*—a spiritual hospital. I was a bit skeptical, but intrigued. We decided to spend forty days and forty nights at the casa and see what happened.

During our time in Brazil, I witnessed what appeared to be miraculous healings, all done faithfully in Jesus' name. A young child who was born deaf began responding to sounds. A woman who had been crippled for decades threw away her canes and walked. A malignant tumor was sliced out of a man's abdomen with a simple kitchen knife and no anesthesia, setting the man free from cancer.

John of God would cruise into a room of prayerful meditators and hopeful patients and announce in Portuguese, "You are all operated on, in the name of Jesus Christ." The healings were very dramatic. But so were the failures. In fact, as in any hospital, spiritual or physical, some of the patients got worse.

My faith in the process was shaky. There was something about putting my trust in John of God, a loud mouthed, cigarette smoking, charismatic leader to bring the healing power of Jesus to me that I didn't fully accept.

I decided to intensify my commitment to seeking out the help of The Great Physician on my own. Every day I sat still in the casa facing a large, commanding painting of Jesus, and prayed: *God, there is something deeply wrong with me. I am unhappy and diseased. I'm in emotional and physical pain all the time. There's no apparent reason for me to be this sick. Sure, I'm disappointed with life and love, but so what? Please tell me how to get well. Please!! I either need to get healed, or just die. I'm sick of being sick.*

It was on the 38th day of consistent daily prayers in this manner that I received a clear answer from God in my heart. "You are suffering from a spiritual deficiency. You do not know who Jesus Christ is. You do not know what your right relationship with Jesus is. All of your suffering comes from this spiritual deficiency."

These words hit me like a ton of bricks. The impact was discombobulating. I *definitely* was spiritually deficient. Something was missing. There was a big, gaping hole in my heart that never got filled no matter how urgently and relentlessly I pursued divine love and ultimate truth. *Could it really be that simple? Was Jesus Christ the answer to all my problems?* I was ready to find out.

Upon our return home to the Big Island of Hawaii, Justice and I once again gave away most of our belongings, packed a tent and a few suitcases, and flew over to the island of Kauai. We had a very strong sense that God was drawing us to the gentle, beautiful garden island to meet Him there. And as it turned out, He was.

.

A Half-Hearted Baptism

Arriving on the island of Kauai felt awkward and strange. My husband and I didn't know how things were laid out, nor did we have any personal contacts. Most clear-minded reasonable people move from one place to another only after they have done quite a bit of due diligence, and have established a substantial support system. We, however, were traveling on a wing and a prayer.

Since there were so many unknowns, we figured the most sensible thing to do was to set up camp at Anini Beach Park. That was to be our home for the first six weeks of this sojourn. With only a vague idea of what we would be doing on Kauai other than seeking the truth, we kept things simple and mobile. God was clearly supporting our pilgrimage with a substantial allowance from a family trust fund.

Justice and I began our spiritual quest on Kauai by regularly attending a very nice congregational church. Hawaiian worship music and practical life lessons were bathed in the sweet spirit of aloha in this tourist-oriented fellowship. The Bible definitely had its place at this church, but the place it had didn't align with the holy order of things that my soul longed for.

"Can we go door to door all over the island and personally invite every single person to attend our church?" I asked the pastor, with a bounce in my voice fueled by my neophyte enthusiasm. "Can we have mid-week, in-depth Bible studies with lots of homework? Can we meet at sunrise each morning for prayer to infuse the day with God's blessings?" My proposals started to take on an outlandishness as I observed the *kahu* (pastor) avoiding my gaze, and distractedly moving some papers around on his desk. I sensed that he was wondering what in the world had happened. He had invited Justice and me to become members of the fellowship, assuming we would be happy with the status quo, and serve the church in ordinary ways that had already been established.

Why was I stirring things up? Did I have to be such a fanatical maniac for God? Couldn't I just calm down and be grateful that there was a lovely Sunday service to attend? Why was my soul still so dissatisfied? Didn't this church represent the Jesus I wanted to serve fully?

I definitely yearned for something meatier. I was craving the T-bone steak of Christianity. The thought occurred to me that maybe if I got baptized I would feel more fulfilled. The only problem was that at that time, I really hadn't accepted Jesus Christ as my Lord and Savior. Surprisingly, however, Kahu didn't consider that a disqualification. He baptized me on the basis that I was *willing to believe* that Jesus Christ was God in the flesh who came into this world as the Messiah. I was open to *having the desire to have the desire* to be a true follower of Christ.

Although my heart was a far cry from where I now believe it should have been to be baptized, this act of commitment turned out to be life-changing for me in a very significant way. Instantaneously, as I emerged from the river, I felt a sense of coming home to myself that was completely new. I was no longer an orphan. I had been adopted into God's personal family. The lonely, scattered wandering of my soul had finally come to

107

an end. I had entered into my inner place of rest.

My outer resting place, a spiritual home here in this world, was still to be found. I desperately longed to be an integral part of a church body that resonated with the depth of my relentless spirit.

Several weeks after my baptism, Justice and I were invited to attend a service at a Calvary Chapel. The spiritual style of this fellowship was so far outside our comfort zone that there is absolutely no way we would have gone there, except for the fact that the pastor was giving a series of sermons on sexual purity. The subject matter was right up our alley. Having both graduated with honors from the excellent, but expensive, school of hard knocks in this very intimate arena, my husband and I were eager to hear what the Bible had to say about sex and chastity.

Without making eye contact with anyone in the congregation, the senior pastor stepped up to the pulpit with maximum intensity. I could tell right away that this was not going to be one of those "feel good," ear-tickling presentations. The mood in this church, at least on this particular Saturday night, was no-nonsense, *whatsoever*. Something was up.

Pastor Bob didn't mince words. He got right to the nitty-gritty about sexual sin on all levels, spelling it out for those who might want to remain in denial. "Wow!" I thought. "This is a *real* church. Jesus' teachings aren't just stored away in a holy book; they're alive!" It was clear that some seriously destructive weeds had crept up in the church garden. Someone was doing something that wasn't right. It didn't take a rocket scientist to figure that one out. But who was it, and what did they do?

At first I wondered, but then I realized that the details

weren't important. What was important was how this church dealt with problems. But even though the corrective mood and language of the message were almost harshly uncompromising, the heart of this pastor for the Lord and His people was overwhelmingly warm, sweet, and genuine. I knew I was sitting in the Father's House.

It was amazing to me how safe and uplifted I felt during the service. The unadulterated truth was being spoken, enveloping me in a protective shield. There was no doubt in my mind. I recognized that voice of the Master coming through the pastor's teachings, and penetrating deep into my heart and soul. It was clearly the Good Shepherd calling me, by name, into the fold. *Welcome Home, Faith! You have sought Me with all of your heart, and you have found Me.*

As compelling and soul-stirring as the message was, amazingly enough, the sermon was not actually the highlight for me. The praise and worship music was the *piece de resistance*. Nothing could have impacted me more. I was immediately transported upward, straight before the throne of grace. This beautiful anointed singing and guitar playing was precisely what my innermost parts had been craving ever since I was a young child. Every note found its way into the longing-filled recesses of my being. I sensed that the heavens had opened up and rained down God's mercy upon me, saturating and refreshing every nook and cranny of who I was.

My voice soared in joyful praise along with the brothers and sisters who, very surprisingly, also loved God in a similar manner. I felt the promise of being the eternal bride of Christ all the way to my bones. Now, here was divine romance at its finest! Once I had tasted this true communion with the Creator of the universe, I knew I was finally Home. Nothing could be more profound and fulfilling for me.

I had been swept off my feet, forever and ever. All I cared about was learning how to increase this intimate encounter with the Lover of my soul.

When I got home from church, I poured through the Bible to absorb myself in the supreme topic of God's love. I started to laugh joyously when I got to John 21: 15-17. Jesus surely was my Teacher. I had been studying all kinds of flowery, exalted, and poetic teachings on love by writers of many paths, but Jesus hit the nail right on the head of my understanding. *"If you love Me, feed My lambs. If you love Me, tend My sheep."* No fluffy sentiment; no lofty ideals. Just love what I love, and serve what I serve. Simple and clear. Yep, I was ready to hang with Jesus.

I kept reading, looking for more juicy words from the Lord of love. There they were in John 15:13: *"Greater love has no one than this, than to lay down one's life for his friends."* Wow! I didn't realize the Bible was filled with one-liners that could knock your socks off and turn your whole world upside down and inside out in the fewest words possible. If I had known that Jesus' style was so punchy and laser-like, I would have started walking with Him a long time ago.

But that was the night the Lord chose to answer many years of fervent prayer for His daughter Faith. The joy and peace I was blessed with were off the charts.

A huge sense of relief welled up in my entire being. I no longer had to navigate my own desperate pursuit of truth or listen to guidance that could not be substantiated. I relaxed into a sweet sense of Homecoming. No more pilgrimaging as a wayfaring stranger, ever again. The Lord was wooing me to Himself with an extravagant love, and I was ready to reciprocate whole-heartedly.

Jesus was not courting Justice with the same gusto as He was courting me at this time. Either that, or my husband simply was not responding with the same passion and relish as I was. I was running with open arms at top speed into Christianity. Justice was backing off. He simply was coming up against too many Christian principles and practices that didn't sit well with him.

Spiritual warfare began to rear its ugly head in our marital relationship.

Sleeping With the Enemy

My newfound joy in Christ was continuously being challenged and resisted as Justice felt me pulling away from ideas, people, and situations that had been deeply meaningful to us as a couple.

As I was attempting to extricate myself from former spiritual beliefs and basically change just about everything I had accepted as truth for decades, Justice, very understandably, would try to reel me back in: "But, *A Course in Miracles* teaches ... Don't you remember what Mother Mary guided us to do? ... He's entering into his Saturn return period. That's why things are getting difficult ... The ascended masters explain that as Christ consciousness...We sacrificed five years of our lives creating all this. You can't just throw it away! ... Their numerology doesn't match up well–not a very promising relationship ... The Bible has been changed so many times..." and on and on.

I was a newborn infant craving the pure milk of the Word in a pristine, supportive environment. Instead, I found myself trying to breathe clearly in what was for me, a highly toxic atmosphere. *How will I ever become strong in the faith? Although certainly not with malicious intent, Justice is nevertheless showing up as the enemy of my soul. This is more than I can bear.*

My realization of how far off Justice and I were from each other came into focus one evening when he asked me to go with him to hear a guest speaker on *A Course in Miracles*.

It's a miracle that I didn't throw up (talk about miracles)

as I witnessed this very attractive middle-aged man elevate and laud himself as a master of miracle manifestation. The entire time he was recounting all the amazing things that were taking place in his life, all I could do was wonder which woman in the group he might be sleeping with. Even the wedding ring on his finger looked suspect. This guy was so obviously playing to the feminine sector, that I felt sorry for his wife, wherever she was—clearly not on Kauai.

By the time the question and answer period was over and Mr. Wonderful's titillating persona was revealed, I knew that the Lord had set this evening up for me to glean a new Biblical perspective on *A Course in Miracles* (a spiritual text that I had not only studied, but taught, for several years). To bear witness to the fruits of such a staunch practitioner of ACIM as this guy was, and to realize that what he represented was quite the opposite of how I wanted to be, was a real eye opener.

My husband, on the other hand, had what was for me, a painfully different experience of the evening. On the way home, Justice decided to get it all out in the open.

"What did you think of that teacher, Faith? He seemed to really know his stuff!"

"Actually, Justice, I thought he was a complete jerk. I didn't trust him one bit, and I felt sick listening to those teachings."

"Well, that's too bad, Faith. Because guess what? That's me! I'm just like that guy. That's who you are married to!" I didn't know specifically what Justice was referring to, but at this point it didn't matter a whole lot. Whatever the connection, I wanted no part of it.

It took me about two weeks to digest this very hard reality. Tension was steadily building in our home.

Finally, one day it all came to a head when my husband and I were at a restaurant with some New Age friends who were visiting us from France. Out of nowhere, Justice started crying uncontrollably. He said he was remembering a past life when he had been chosen as a human sacrifice to jump into the volcanic cauldron on the Big Island of Hawaii. According to this story, which was very real to him, I had also been his wife in that lifetime, and after his death, I immediately went off with another man (who was now, in this life, a prominent spiritual leader in the church we were attending). Our New Age friends confirmed that this was an accurate account, and I was the recalcitrant, not accepting reality. They insisted that I was in denial.

By the time we returned home from the restaurant, the Lord had spoken to me. These people, *including my husband*, were possessed by dark spirits. I basically threw our guests out of our home after having a huge argument with them, and the Great Wall of China erected itself unbidden between Justice and me. This had gone too far. I no longer could tolerate dealing with such a deep level of delusion coming at me continually. I was being held accountable for what my husband fully believed I had done in past lives, and what he had calculated and projected about me and my relationships based on the stars and numbers in this life. I literally could barely breathe in this atmosphere.

A devastating spiritual battle was taking place in my home; the very place that I needed as a refuge. The standard "Home Sweet Home" placard above the mantle had been replaced with the sobering message: "*For we do not wrestle against flesh and blood, but against principalities, against powers, against the rulers of the darkness of this age, against spiritual hosts of wickedness in the heavenly places*" (Ephesians 6:12). I discovered that from a spiritual perspective, I truly was sleeping with the enemy.

Consecrated Lives

By God's amazing grace, Justice was aware that something just wasn't right inside of him. He sought help from the pastors and elders of the church we were attending. Over a period of months, my husband was prayed over, anointed, and counseled, and remarkable changes occurred. The constant, disruptive onslaughts abated and were replaced with a gentler spirit of understanding. I was freed up to pursue the Lord wholeheartedly. Justice happily came alongside me as a loving and willing support. Together, "holy living" became our credo, as well as our email address.

As Justice and I both followed the upward call of Christ and walked away from our eclectic spiritual pasts, we were called upon to do something radical; a good old fashioned book burning.

In our possession were 300 copies of the channeled book (dictated by the spirit who presented herself as Mother Mary) that we had published entitled *The Man Woman Dilemma/ Relationship Truths for Troubled Times*. After calculating the cost, and with the help of twenty other people from our church fellowship, we tossed each book on a blazing funeral pyre. This was the death of our "baby."

I imagined that I would be traumatized and devastated as I watched our five-year labor of love go up in flames, but that was not the case. That holy fire was a refining one, not a consuming one. It left me with a sweet taste of freedom. The Son had set me free, and I was free, indeed.

When there was nothing left of our books but a heap of ashes, Justice and I were poised for a complete renewing of our minds. But there was a major force blocking this process. We both found ourselves entangled in a seemingly endless maze of beliefs that somehow (supernaturally) needed to be unwound. It was like trying to straighten out a confused mass of spaghetti that had been hardening and sticking together in a huge pot for a very long time. The hungrier I got, the more determined I was to break through to my soul's destination.

The Final Step

One of my feet was on the gas; I had decided to follow Jesus. The other foot was on the brakes; I still held some gripping core beliefs that were at odds with Christianity. With such double-mindedness living inside of me, I wasn't really going anywhere. True, I had made a strong external commitment, but my heart and soul were not fully on board. For all intents and purposes, I was identifying myself as a Messianic Jew, a believer in Christ, but that was not enough. I knew I had to take the final step.

That final step was to pray a sincere, fervent prayer from the bottom of my heart that would call forth the needed medicine and sanctification for every part of my being that was not in full alignment with God's heart. In other words, I needed to cry out for the truth, the whole truth, and nothing but the truth, at all costs.

I checked out the master prayer warriors for inspiration. David's Psalm 139 became the launching pad for my own heart cry that opened the gates of heaven to usher me into a complete and utterly fulfilling conversion.

David's prayer:

Search me, O God, and know my heart: Try me and know my anxieties; and see if there is any wicked [twisted] way in me, and lead me in the way everlasting (Psalm 139:23-24).

Faith's prayer:

Lord God, You know everything that I am made of. If there are any desires, ideas, beliefs, practices, habits, ways, attachments or inclinations that are in me that are not of You, please remove or redeem them, no matter how painful the process might be for me. I want to be purely holy and a vital, useful instrument for Your kingdom work. Dear God, reform and fashion me in to the image of Your Son. Place me firmly on the narrow path leading straight into Your heart.

As I had been learning, the Lord often responds to the prayers of His saints with revelations and instruction. I was not expecting some magic-genie kind of response to my outpourings. There was no expectation that I would wake up one morning and miraculously find myself clear as a bell and free from all ungodly thoughts, feelings, and attachments. No, I was going to have to face head-on what was holding me back in my relationship with the Lord, and take some strong action to pursue a deeper and purer knowledge of Him.

By taking the final step, I had burned my boats and my bridges, once and for all. There was absolutely no turning back. My face was set like a flint towards my spiritual Home in Christ.

Food, Glorious Food!

The first and foremost unreconciled issue that I knew was hindering my intimacy with the Lord concerned food. I had some major misunderstandings about the relationship between physical food and spirituality. Not only were my beliefs in this area confused, but I was engaged in a constant struggle to gain self-control over what I put into my mouth.

As far back as I could remember into my early childhood, my relationship with food was unhealthy and problematic. Instead of eating to live, I lived to eat. What I ate was not only for sustenance and enjoyment, but food substituted as a salve for my broken heart and nourishment for my longing spirit. Because I was hungering for spiritual food, but I was settling for material food, I was always left unsatisfied, lustily wanting more.

Ruled by the stomach, there was not much room for a sovereign Lord in my life. I already had a rigorous master. Gluttony, like all other fleshly compulsions, can easily become all consuming. Life was what I did in between meals and snacks.

Because the pride of life was even a stronger force in me than the relentless pull to satisfy my tongue and stomach, the battle of the bulge stayed well within certain parameters. I never did become the 200-pounder I probably would have been if image and bodily comfort had not been such strong influences on my appetite. But regardless of the effective stops, I have certainly been a sorrowful slave to the demands of this body.

When I first entered the Hindu ashram at age 23, I seriously hoped that the strict, regulated vegetarian diet would quell my gluttonous tendencies. Not so! Ironically, my eating spun more out of control than ever. Because I was not one of the ashram cooks, I didn't have regular access to the kitchen. The only food available to me was the delicious fare that was served at meal times. This type of restricted eating doesn't work so well for an unhealed glutton.

Sneaking into the temple kitchen late at night when everyone was asleep became a regular part of my schedule. I would grab whatever I could get my hands on, even devouring foods that I didn't particularly like. My spirit was so compromised and thankless that I gained 35 pounds before the year was out. Something *really* wasn't getting fed properly, deep inside of me.

An ongoing battle presented itself day after day for quite some time. Not only was I putting on weight, but I was losing vitality. The doctors were telling me I needed to eat meat and drink some wine to nourish and balance my body properly. My guru was telling me (based on the ancient teachings of the Vedas, the holy books of India) that being a squeaky-clean vegetarian is the first and most fundamental step on the spiritual path; that our eternal glorified bodies are prepared in this life by a pure vegetarian lifestyle. In fact, according to that way of thinking, one must be a vegetarian in order to develop the finer brain substance that allows you to even begin to understand the perfect, exalted nature of God.

What I discovered many years later, however, was that this teaching, as beautiful as it sounded, was built on a faulty foundation. God cannot be known or understood with our brains. He comes to us through revelation, from His warm, loving heart to ours. The Lord does not require us to develop super crystal clear brains by following certain restrictive diets, in order to know Him. In fact, His ways fly in the face of this erroneous proposal.

Have you ever met unrefined country folk who can barely read or speak intelligently, but are clearly beaming the pure light of God's love? The Lord uses the simple things of this world to *"confound the wise"* (1 Corinthians 2:27). He does this just to make sure we get it—that there is nothing we need do, or can do, to lift ourselves up to receive the grace of His personal revelation into our lives. It is always a free gift, not a scientific formula.

When I was in the ashram, following the Vedic teachings of my guru, I fully believed that not only was vegetarianism the beginning of true spirituality, but also that the killing and eating of animals caused humans to become violent, hard-headed, uncompassionate, and untrustworthy. I was absolutely convinced for over 25 years that the Bible was a very sketchy body of knowledge simply because much of it was scribed by meat-eaters.

I never questioned the ideas I held sacred about food and spirituality at all until our Hindu monastery moved to Three Rivers, a small mountain town in the San Joaquin Valley of California. The population was predominantly Christian. It didn't take very long before a very humbling and rather shocking thing happened. I discovered that my conclusions about carnivores were fallacious. Almost all of the townspeople I met were remarkably kind, gentle, and caring. There was a warmth and generosity of spirit to these Christians that was missing in most of the Hindu monastics whom I was accustomed to being with. So, the undeniable evidence was presented to me. Vegetarianism was not the dividing line between the godly and the ungodly, as I had contended for so long. There was a higher law of God that was the determining factor.

That higher law, I was happy to find out, is the law of love. This beautiful law is meant to govern every aspect of our lives, including food. When I finally did read the Bible with an open mind and heart, the verse which best explained for me the principle underlying the wisest, most godly food choices was Romans 14:20: *"Do not tear down the work of God for the sake of food. All things indeed are pure, but it is evil for the man who eats with offense. It is good neither to eat meat nor drink wine nor do anything by which your brother stumbles or is offended or is made weak."*

Okay. Now this was making perfect sense. Food is not really the issue. Relationship is the issue. If my relationship with my brother or sister lacks love, *that* is the stumbling block on the spiritual path. Especially when we are seated together at the Lord's Table.

To deepen my new understanding, I did a little more research. *"Not what goes into the mouth defiles a man; but what comes out of the mouth, this defiles a man"* (Matthew 15:11). Those words of Jesus seemed to pop right off the page and penetrate into my heart of hearts as unadulterated truth. The ingesting of meat, fish, eggs, coffee, tea, wine, or anything else I had abstained from for most of my adult life, would not create distance between me and God. The speaking of inconsiderate, hurtful things to my neighbor would. If I was unsettled with my eating habits, the difficulties were truly not with my stomach or my tongue. The real issues were to be found in my heart, the wellspring of all my outward expressions.

A huge hole got punched in the self-righteous bubble I had created for myself. We vegetarians considered ourselves an exclusive, favored group of spiritually advanced, mature lovers of God. How humbling it was to find out that God invites us to eat and enjoy all the sumptuous foods He created for human consumption! All He asks is that we do it for His glory and with thankful hearts. *Food, glorious food!*

Of course there are times and circumstances when a light vegetarian diet can be extremely helpful. In the book of Daniel, this Old Testament prophet and his friends went on a ten day diet of vegetables and water, which resulted in remarkable blessings. Their countenances were clear and bright, *"And in all matter of wisdom and understanding about which the king examined them, he found them ten times better than all the magicians and astrologers who were in all his realm"* (Daniel 1:20).

So just as an athlete might go on a high carb diet before a race to maximize his performance, we might choose to eat vegetarian or even fast for specific purposes. But there is certainly no compulsion to do so by God. The godly prescription for food is this: Choose freely, eat gratefully, and love your brothers and your sisters more than the food. Learning these truths brought me many steps closer to a total immersion into the Christian way of life. Many of the "Yes, buts" were eliminated.

Sheep in Wolves' Clothing

The #2 unresolved issue that took its toll on my ability to fully dive into Christianity was the question of modesty. According to my understanding, a restrained and moderate presentation was fundamental to true godliness.

Modesty is an interesting point to consider because what is seen as modest in one culture, at a certain time or in a certain circumstance, may be interpreted as completely immodest in another culture, at another time or another circumstance.

My perspective on modesty had been well defined in the Krishna ashrams. All forms of shy and decorous attitudes were held up as the most prized virtues for women. Our dress code was very specific. We wore saris that draped our bodies from head to toe, and our long, uncut locks were bound up and covered. Loose hair was considered an outward indication of loose morals, and visible flesh above the ankles was seen askance as blatantly seductive. According to this Vedic standard, no godly woman would risk her chaste standing in the community to conform to worldly styles.

Not only was our outward appearance strictly regulated to uphold these standards of modesty, but our inner qualities and behavior, as well. Cultivating shyness, quietness, calmness, and demureness were part of my daily spiritual practices as a monastic woman, and also learning to mince my words, glances, and steps. In this regard, the training that I received was tantamount to attending a highly refined finishing school. My inner and outer being were redesigned and shaped to be "pleasing to God" and "suitable to man," according to the guidelines set forth in the Vedas.

The other rigid protocols that were taught to the women to insure modesty, and hopefully, to provide a sense of honoring and safety for both the men and the women, were strict limitations on how we connected with members of the opposite sex. Unless communications were absolutely unavoidable, I did not look at or speak to men other than my husband.

Over the years, I actually became so uptight and awkward around men that I tried to steer clear of them, at all costs. On occasion, when I did have important business with a man, I would keep my eyes cast downward as we conversed. Talking was one thing. Looking was another.

Unfortunately, what resulted from all these preventative measures was not true modesty, but a distorted, almost neurotic sense of relationship. Concern about distracting my brothers from their pure spiritual focus became all-consuming for me rather than embracing these wonderful men with warm sisterly love and respect. I was worshiping at the altar of a god of fear, not the true God who is love.

Did all these attempts at maintaining modesty and chastity even work to produce the desired results of keeping the lust of the flesh and lust of the eyes in check? Not really. As my sinful nature would have it, I found myself irresistibly drawn to one of the temple *sannyasis* (a single monk who had taken lifetime vows of celibacy). Even though my outward behavior was modest towards him, my heart and mind were not. No matter how willing I was to submit myself to a bit and bridle corralling of my senses, my inner being was yearning for something forbidden.

Towards the end of my 20 years of ashram life, I had an awful realization. Although the standards of modesty worked very naturally in the Indian culture, when they were translated into this culture, they became distorted. The truth was, I was losing touch with myself as a woman. My wild and passionate nature had been denied and stifled for so long by the strict regulations of the Krishna path, that I was actually becoming emotionally unhealthy.

I decided to cut myself some slack. *Who will it harm if I cut loose in the privacy of my own home? God sees me when I'm naked. He certainly can handle me in a pair of skimpy shorts and a tank top!* So I went shopping, donned my meager attire, and let it rip. With Olatunji, Drums of Passion, playing in the background, I revived that primal part of me that had been hidden and subdued for over two decades.

My oldest son, Matt, who was ten years old at the time, and had never seen my bare legs or my undraped torso, happened to come home while I was dancing with wild abandon. "*Mom!! What* are *you* doing??" he cried in a horrified voice. The shock on his face told me that not only had his eyes been wounded by this unexplainable, outrageous scene, but his heart and soul, as well. He no longer felt safe. Based on everything that Matt had learned from the time of his birth, his mother had succumbed to the dark, enticing ways of the world. I was no longer a person he could trust.

Despite the fact that my new presentation began to cause unrest at home, there was no turning back for me. A spark of aliveness had been reignited, and at that point, I could care less about modesty. Glamour and independence quickly replaced propriety and submission in my value system, and I chose to pursue this new exciting path full-on. In fact, I wrote a country western song that expressed my very modern, worldly attitude: *"I'm a my-way-or-the-highway kind of lady, I'm a my-way-or-the-highway kind of girl. I am here today, but I'll be gone by Friday..."* Fortunately, I sang the song mostly to myself.

Following the women's lib mood of the day, the pendulum swung quickly to the opposite end of the spectrum from where I had lived most of my adult life. Not only did I unwind my braids and let my hair flow freely, but I highlighted my hair very blonde. As if that wasn't enough of a radical change, I went the full nine yards with breast implants, thinking that not only did blondes have more fun, but that voluptuous blondes had the most fun. I was right ... for a very short time, that is.

Six years later I found myself back in the hospital having the breast implants removed. Not only was I seriously ill with an autoimmune disease that was linked to foreign bodies being in my system, but I was emotionally distraught. I was definitely attracting lots of attention, but it was the wrong kind of attention. I no longer had any privacy. My feminine inner being always felt violated. My heart and soul were being eclipsed by my body. The immodest, ungodly approach to life was backfiring, as it always does, and always will.

It was not until many years later when I started to attend Christian churches fairly regularly that the issue of modesty surfaced again in ways that created major spiritual confusion for me, and a serious road block in my ability to fully embrace Christianity. Justice and I found a wonderful church, with great worship music and powerful, anointed sermons, but from the minute we walked inside the building (supposedly the sanctuary, but far from a safe haven in our opinions) until the minute we left, my dear husband had to keep his eyes closed so as not to be distracted by enticingly clad females who seemed to be wearing fashions designed by Satan.

Something didn't compute. This was clearly God's family, loving and serving Him. The presence of the Holy Spirit in the congregation was palpable. But so was the appearance of evil. *Would these women dress like that if they really knew that Jesus was there, in their midst? Are the men so desensitized by the world's styles and standards that they don't recognize that their wives, daughters, and sisters are dressing inappropriately and indecently? Or am I still in culture shock from my monastery background, and unable to see holiness and purity beyond the miniskirts and cleavage oriented tops?*

As I recognized that I was allowing myself to judge others by external appearances and thus distance myself from actually being present with the Lord, the Holy Spirit would convict me. Over and over, as I was thinking, *Yikes! I can't believe she's wearing that! I'm shocked that that is showing! What kind of church is this, anyway? Can I really make this my place of worship?* The very person whom I was labeling and judging would express his or her intimate, sweet love and devotion to Jesus in such a beautiful way that I would be humbled. If I was seeing things as impure, that was really my problem, not anyone else's. (*"To the pure all things are pure..."* Titus 1:15). I decided to mind my own business and just worship the Lord. What freedom!

I was also reminded that the Father purposely placed the forbidden fruit right smack in the center of the Garden of Eden. Adam and Eve had to contend with their sinful natures and be accountable for their choices. The original sanctuary was not devoid of temptation, and neither is the Lord's church. Expecting a congregation of godly people to look, act, and speak according to my understanding of what a disciple of Jesus Christ is like is absurd. James cautioned the early church members against this very tendency: "*Who are you to judge another?*" (James 4:12b).

Besides, Jesus is the Great Physician. Physicians don't come to minister to the healthy. They come to heal the sick. His church is meant to be a place of fervent prayer and a spiritual hospital, not a high-class, stately congregation hall. Of course, the people who come to worship are going to exhibit different symptoms, but everyone will be needy in some noticeable way. Some may have more healing to do in the arena of modesty than others, but when the Lord looks upon His children, He is not focusing on our flesh. He is looking into our hearts.

Humble hearts and contrite spirits are the raw ingredients of holy beauty and true modesty, much more so than outward appearances.

So, if you happen to run into me, Faith Collier, in person, you might actually see me comfortably wearing a pair of tight fitting jeans—even in church! Hallelujah. I am clothed in the righteousness of Christ. I believe that His definition of modesty is simply to be moderate and unassuming.

The Biblical guidelines on modesty are certainly not meant to draw lines between the godly and the ungodly. They are reminders that our lives are designed by the Creator to be living sacrifices. The divine order of things is God first, others second, me last. Once again, the Laws of Love reign supreme. Our presence ought to leave a sweet aroma of Christ, not a bitter aftertaste that makes others wish we had stayed home!

In the process of learning what modesty is and what modesty isn't, and relating this all back to Jesus and the church, I find myself very grateful that our Lord hobnobbed with prostitutes, thieves, and the like. When He was speaking to the woman caught in adultery, for instance, He did not tell her to go and stop dyeing her hair, painting her nails, and wearing inappropriate attire. Rather He stated simply and directly the real problem at hand; *"Neither do I condemn you; go and sin no more."* (John 8:11). Sin is the separating factor between man and God, not personal style, social standing, or anything else.

So gradually, over the years of worshiping and serving alongside the saints, I have come to understand that God's family is a motley crew. He has called queens to Himself, and streetwalkers. He has called fashion models and ragamuffins. He has called the mature and the immature. Different cultures are merging together as one in the house of the Lord. What a colorful, fascinating environment to learn to love and honor our brothers and sisters right where they are.

Thus I have come to peace with the general lack of modesty among many Christians, and no longer use this issue as an excuse to keep my distance. With this concern laid to rest, I found myself facing one more major stumbling block. And, it has been a really big one...

Come Again?

Up until a few years ago, I believed in reincarnation without question. I assumed it was a fact of nature, just like the law of gravity. Pretty much everyone I knew worldwide also believed in reincarnation, so there was no reason at all for me to try to unlock this strong doctrine from my consciousness. A very mystical feeling accompanied my belief in reincarnation. Whatever situation I found myself in seemed to be inextricably connected to the far-reaching, unknowable past and the many possibilities for the future.

An endless web of speculative dramas and convoluted relationships was set up in my mind, always wondering if I had been someone's daughter, husband, teacher, or enemy in a past life, and what would be our relationship in the life to come, especially if there was a sense of familiarity or deja-vu that we experienced together. Sometimes I even sought out astrological, numerological, or psychic readings to provide background information that would help explain why things happened the way they did, and felt the way they felt.

Situations became multi-dimensional, seeming to be the good or bad consequences of choices made by my soul when it was incarnated in different bodies. This very complicated way of viewing life proved to be exhausting. If I had truly been through 8,400,000 incarnations, as I was taught by the holy books of India, it certainly was time to finish up my business here on this planet, and get out, once and for all.

There must be some kind of way out of here frequently ran through my brain, as I continually heard echoes of Jimi Hendrix and Bob Dylan crying out for resolution and rest. I certainly was in the same boat with these soul-wrenched men, and was heavy-laden with a strong sense of past lives that I believed in, but couldn't quite put my finger on. When I had been in the Hindu ashram, my guru supposedly had delivered me from all the karmas of past lives and graced me into eternal freedom with God, but the fascination that I had developed for knowing the past and the future kept me bound up in delusion.

As I shared earlier in this book, there was a radical occurrence that took place that shook me out of 40 years of clinging staunchly to the doctrine of reincarnation. That was when my husband, Justice, fell apart without warning one day at a restaurant, convinced that he was remembering a past life when he had been chosen by the Hawaiian king as a human sacrifice to jump off into the volcanic cauldron. This whole incident was so sickening to me that I was forced to reevaluate my ideas. Believing in reincarnation had always complicated things to some degree, but then it began causing serious problems.

I found out that the Bible teaches that there is only one lifetime for man. This concept seemed very simplistic and hard to grasp, for someone like me who was thinking in more cosmic terms. But as I prayed about this, a soothing peace came over me. A huge burden was lifted. My understanding of life and death became real and grounded, rather than vague and universal. Accepting the Word of God narrowed my attention to what was right in front of me.

What if I took birth just to love God and love people right now, today, in this present moment of divine opportunity? What if the only future I need to think about is worshipping eternally with the saints and angels in heaven? What if the only reason to look back is to testify to the Lord's transforming grace upon me?

The time had definitely come to release the "many lives" theory that I had embraced wholeheartedly for so long. I was going to need a lot of faith to get through this one. It was like discovering that the earth is round after believing from day one that it was flat.

God decided to help me learn more about faith first hand. Here's what happened.

I was at a church gathering and chose to sit down next to a lovely, soft-spoken elderly woman who was visiting from out of town. She turned out to be the mother-in-law of a pastor I knew. Out of the blue, Lorraine touched my shoulder, moved in very close to me as if I were her most intimate friend, and began to speak tenderly.

"Don't you ever just wonder if any of this is true, Faith?"

"Any of what, Lorraine?"

"You know, all this stuff about Jesus and the Bible."

It took me a few breaths before I could respond. I knew Lorraine's children and grandchildren, and they had all been blessed beautifully by her in the faith. "You mean you think that maybe we're all mistaken?"

"Well, no. Not really. But sometimes, you just have to wonder. You know what I mean, right?"

Actually, I did. I knew what it meant that, this side of heaven, all we can rely on is our faith. I knew what it was like to have that faith severely tested.

With these ideas ruminating in my mind, and prayers for Lorraine saturating my heart, I returned home and prayed to be led to some Bible verses that could help me strengthen my faith and apply that faith to my unresolved situation. What could be more perfect than reading about the inspiring mountain movers in the book of Hebrews who fully received the free gift of faith and walked in it. *"By faith Abel ... by faith Enoch ... by faith Noah... by faith Abraham ... by faith Sarah..."* (Hebrews 11:4-12). And now I was clearly being asked to step forward in the same manner: By faith, Faith...

And so it was that I was delivered from the last major stronghold that was sidetracking me off the straight and narrow path. I was set free to commune with God purely and simply. There was no longer any curiosity about who I had been and who I will become, other than that I was lost and now I'm found; that I was blind and now I see; that I was a desperate pilgrim, and now I am betrothed to become the eternal bride of Christ.

Home at Last

Remember the beautiful red cardinal that I wrote about in the beginning of this book that kept bashing itself into the transparent walls of my all-glass greenhouse kitchen, trying to fly freely towards the beautiful mountains and open sky? Well, I think you will understand now why that bird and I had a lot in common. We both were caught in misguided, illusory traps that nearly killed us.

By God's grace, for both my feathery friend and myself, there was a way out through the open door. Could the cardinal have picked itself up off the floor after it was severely bruised and its energy spent, and found its way back out to its home in the sky? No. It surely would have died, having been exhausted and beaten up by countless enervating attempts at the impossible. Only because it had come to the end of itself was it vulnerable enough for me to intercede, lift it up, and carry it to the path of freedom.

In the same way, the road that I was traveling, seeking for the true Light in spiritual teachings and practices that were impure, would never have taken me to my heavenly destination. The anguish and despair that I was experiencing, persistently pursuing God in religions and belief systems that were like broken cisterns, unable to hold the quickened living waters that could quench the thirst of my parched soul, finally weakened me to the point where I was able and willing to be ushered through the Door to ultimate freedom.

Here is the deeper meaning of "*The Lesson of the Cardinal*" that was revealed to me immediately after the greenhouse incident took place. This was not an ordinary occurrence.

That morning, I had sensed a strong prompting by the Holy Spirit to begin writing this book. I looked to Jesus as the author and teacher of all messages worth disseminating. Since the Master used parables in His communications, it was my desire to use parables in mine. I tend to be unpoetic and rather direct, so I was at a complete loss how to create a metaphorical story that would capture the essence and purport of my spiritual journey.

By lunch time, the divinely orchestrated event that set the stage for the "*Lesson of the Cardinal*" parable literally took place. Then the revelation was given.

Lesson of the Cardinal Explained

Bold statements drawn from Chapter 1 of this book

"A beautiful red cardinal flew into my all-glass greenhouse kitchen through the open door one day while I was preparing lunch."

The beautiful red cardinal is the sincere truth seeker. The purity and richness of this bird's scarlet plumage represent the devoted heart and relentless spirit of one who quests for truth.

"As the bird viewed the mountains, trees, and sky through the glass walls, it naturally tried to return to the great outdoors by flying straight towards the wonderful scenery."

It is instinctive for birds to fly through the sky, soaring freely in the beauty of nature. Similarly, God has placed eternity in the hearts of men (Ecclesiastes 3:11). We are designed to yearn for and move towards our true Home in the eternal kingdom. Mankind is meant to respond wholeheartedly to that upward call.

"But the cardinal didn't realize there was an impenetrable, invisible barrier preventing it from reaching its desired destination."

The impediments and stumbling blocks on the spiritual path are subtle, but formidable. Birds cannot discern invisible barriers, and neither can men, unless our eyes are anointed with heavenly unction (the Lord's grace). In a condition of spiritual blindness, it is entirely possible to be going a hundred miles an hour in the wrong direction and not perceive any impending danger.

"Thus it repeatedly bashed itself against the transparent

walls, duped and misguided by the *illusion of freedom*."

The glass greenhouse is the world of religious doctrine and spiritual practice. Just as the cardinal was free to fly in and have a look around, so too are we given free will to explore and taste the smorgasbord of transcendental possibilities. However, what appears to be a banquet hall often becomes a prison for our souls.

"I reached out in an attempt to direct the confused, enervated bird towards the only way to true freedom, the open door, but in its fearful, desperate state, the cardinal saw my extended hand as a threat."

God's ambassadors of loving kindness are reaching out to direct us to the way of deliverance. As the cardinal misinterpreted my life-giving gesture, even so, many truth seekers commit the cardinal sin of not recognizing their Messiah and His messengers.

"Rather than receiving my help, the poor bird thrust itself even harder and faster at the clear greenhouse walls."

Once the outstretched hand of Christ is rejected, the scrambling process begins. The lack of soul-satisfaction drives the desperate pilgrim deeper and wider into anything that promises peace and happiness. This new healing modality; that new workshop. This new revelation; that new relationship. Hitting the wall is the painful outcome that is meant to be a wake-up call. *The Door is over here. Be free. Come Home!*

"Finally, it came to the end of itself and fell to the floor completely spent and broken."

The seeker faces the devastating reality that "*This also is vanity and grasping for the wind*" (Ecclesiastes 6:9). The brokenness that he has been trying to run from, humbles him and takes him down. It is in this selfless, vulnerable state that the

140

soul-wrenched pilgrim becomes available to receive the Lord's healing grace.

"At this point, I was able to pick up the beautiful red cardinal, carry it outside through the open door, and gently place it on a tree."

Jesus, the Good Shepherd, relates a parable with a similar message. "*What man of you, having a hundred sheep, if he loses one of them, does not leave the ninety-nine in the wilderness, and go after the one which is lost until he finds it? And when he has found it, he lays it on his shoulders, rejoicing*" (Luke 15:5).

Our Lord is gentle and personal. He loves and cares for His sheep. God's Son has come "*to preach good tidings to the poor...to heal the brokenhearted. To proclaim liberty to the captives, and the opening of the prison to those who are bound... To give them beauty for ashes, the oil of joy for mourning, the garment of praise for the spirit of heaviness; that they may be called trees of righteousness, the planting of the LORD, that He may be glorified*" (Isaiah 61:1-3).

What hopeless person, hitting bottom, wouldn't want to be picked up, carried outside to freedom, and gently placed in a refuge where he will be ministered to by the Great Physician? This is an absolute miracle of love that truly is available to everyone.

The open door that is mentioned in this part of the parable is also very significant. In John 10:9 Jesus states, "*I am the door. If anyone enters by Me, he will be saved, and will go in and out and find pasture.*" The beautiful red cardinal had only one way out of the greenhouse; through the open door. Similarly, there was only one way out of the soupy, messed up spiritual predicament I had foolishly fallen into, over and over again. Through the open door—Yeshua, Messiah.

Jeanne Guyon, a well-known Christian saint, wrote these exquisite words from her prison cell in St. Antoine, France, many years ago: "Oh, the unspeakable happiness of belonging to Jesus Christ! Belonging to Jesus Christ is the true balm which sweetens all those pains and sorrows which are so inseparable from this earthly life." (*Experiencing the Depths of Jesus Christ* by Jeanne Guyon).

It is the blessed truth of belonging *to* Him, abiding *in* Him, and living *for* Him that has ended my relentless, desperate pilgrimage. I am *Home At Last.*

Afterword

"In My Father's house are many mansions; if it were not so, I would have told you. I go to prepare a place for you. And if I go and prepare a place for you, I will come again and receive you to Myself; that where I am, there you may be also" (John 14:2-3).

The Lord has been giving me a longing, a taste, and a glimpse each day of the wondrous place He is preparing for me in heaven.

I currently live and serve in an environment that continuously takes my breath away. Majestic mountains, sculpted ponds, waterfalls, royal palm trees, tropical gardens, and exotic fragrances provide an extravagant backdrop for the "Private Sanctuary" ministry to which God has called me. How this property came to be my home and mission field is truly a miracle of grace.

Several years ago, my husband and I moved out of the condo we were leasing into a tent. Condo living was grating on my nerves. Cars were revving up in the parking lot outside our window before the break of dawn, and neighbors were working out their family dynamics in loud-pitched voices right behind my living room wall. Camping out in nature seemed like the logical antidote.

When tent-living lost its charm during the rainy season, Justice and I decided to look for more substantial accommodations. We joined the ranks of homeless-by-choice people who were half-heartedly thrust into the Kauai housing market. The really nice places, which were few and far between, were way outside our means. The affordable ones, which were also few and far between, were uninspiring. As I prayed about our situation, I heard a very clear directive: "Do not look for a place to live. No need to check the paper, Craig's list, or the real estate offices. Your new home will show up as a miracle."

Shortly thereafter, Justice and I were at a local gathering with people we had gotten to know quite intimately in just a couple of weeks. I mentioned that we were living in a tent, and wondering where our next home would be. Before the group dispersed, one woman, who I especially liked, approached me with a light, playful invitation. "Come in my car," she said smiling quite irresistibly. "I want to show you something."

The Lexus we were driving in pulled into a multi-million dollar, highly landscaped estate property. My jaw dropped. This was as close to heaven on earth as any place I had ever seen, here or abroad. Our delightful new friend continued, "My husband owns this property. How would you two like to live here?" Justice and I looked at one another. *What does she mean,* **live here**? *Maybe people with this level of affluence can't begin to relate to the fact that renting such a place as this would wipe us out financially in no time.*

"Really?" I asked quizzically. You are inviting us to live here? What do we need to do to make this work for you and your husband?"

"Nothing," Joan responded simply. "Just take care of it, and use it for good." That was eight years ago.

To this day, we steward the Sanctuary as a refuge for those who are seeking to draw near to the Lord. Over the years, the Holy Spirit has sent grievers, honeymooners, ex-convicts, divorcees, pastors, backpackers, widows, orphans, people in recovery, college students, and pilgrims. We pray; they come. It's really that simple and wonderful.

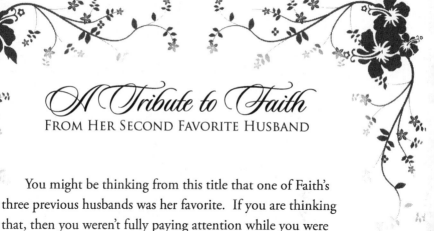

A Tribute to Faith
FROM HER SECOND FAVORITE HUSBAND

You might be thinking from this title that one of Faith's three previous husbands was her favorite. If you are thinking that, then you weren't fully paying attention while you were reading this book and getting to know Faith.

At times I have done the same thing—gotten caught up in the momentary story and my own interpretations of situations and circumstances—and lost sight of who Faith truly is. But that confusion doesn't last for long. Faith's character and qualities don't allow for such lapses. When someone continues to shine brightly even in the midst of a dark storm; when all the electricity has gone out for everyone else but there continues to be this powerful transformer emitting a light that just won't go out, then you have some idea of who Faith is. Relentless is a very good word to describe her.

The amazing thing is that this torch can range from burning extremely hot and fiery to emanating a beautiful, soft, glowing radiance, all the way to bouncing along with an effervescent delightfulness; yet all coming from the same Source and with the ability to change just like that (a snap of the fingers)! I believe this is one of the things that Faith demonstrates best—what it is to be child*like* without being child*ish*.

The feminine nature is usually recognized as being flowing, like water. But, as I understand it, the Holy Spirit came to baptize with fire. Since water always seeks the lowest level,

God has steam-cleaned Faith in a way that the lower watery nature has been vaporized allowing for the fiery light of His truth to shine clearly, yet resiliently, through her radiant countenance (or is it His Countenance?). Often in my boyish way of pushing against things to feel some sense of power, I can't tell whether it's Faith I'm up against, or the Lord, Himself.

The other morning while my wife and I were praying in our little outdoor chapel, an image of the Statue of Liberty flashed in my mind. This is Faith. She holds up this light, this torch, so that others can see the liberty that is available. She doesn't harp on people, or beat a dead drum, or proselytize, or make altar calls. That's not who she is. She just stands there, straight and tall for all to see, and holds the light of God's truth, and the promise of eternal salvation.

Don't get me wrong. Faith is not made of stone like a statue. In fact, quite the contrary. She feels everyone deeply. She knows what's going on with them. Her heart breaks for the sufferings of others. But, because she understands that the only real help comes from above, all she can rightfully do is to stand tall in the truth of her own freedom, peace, and joy and point to where all this grace came from.

At the Sanctuary where we live, that's what Faith does. God brings the tired and the poor—those who are in need of soul-level healing—and Faith holds this high light of truth in the way she lives and relates. That salt-of-the-earth light either attracts people closer to it or they shade their eyes and withdraw. Oh, some try to manipulate or dominate or contend in one way or another, but that doesn't last very long. Faith's genuine extension of the Lord's love and grace and forgiveness is *very* disarming. So, people with personal agendas discover that they can't run their normal *shtick* (a Yiddish word that means

146

one's signature behavior or the way that their personality has developed to get what they want). They soon realize that they too have to surrender to the Lord Jesus Christ, or go run their *shtick* somewhere else… where it still works.

As you can well imagine, being married to Faith is not easy. Sometimes I actually hate it because this remarkable woman makes me face myself at levels deeper than I want to go. The root of Faith's stance is *chutzpah*, an iron will that is grounded in the Will of God. The truth that Faith stands in doesn't even need words. It forebears. It feeds. It extends a gentle hand. When I'm ready to blast people for their transgressions, she caresses them with words of truth that are so high, so soft, and so brilliant that the offenders don't even know they've been chastised. Rather than resisting correction, they supernaturally start moving in the right direction! It's astonishing.

I've heard it said that the only real impediment to the truth is the belief that you already have it. Faith's testimony is an excellent demonstration of non-attachment to everything that proved fruitless in order to find and live the ultimate truth. Whenever she needed to unhinge and make a course correction, she did.

If there are lessons to be drawn from this book, first of all I pray that you've extracted them on your own; that you've received the inspiration that you need and have the courage to keep moving towards your ultimate Home in Christ. The only thing I'd add is a strong invitation to pay attention to the amazing power of a Godly woman.

What I see has happened with lots of females—from the woman's lib movement, to the New Spirituality, and even into the Christian Church—is that they have attempted to "take their power back" from men. From entering the boardrooms and competing on the same turf, to becoming "goddesses" alongside their "godly" cohorts, to mimicking the masculine authority from the pulpit, women have incorrectly surmised that their power has everything to do with the men who they think have usurped it.

But Faith is an excellent example that a woman's true beauty and power are found in an unwavering devotion to God in her *feminine* calling. Like the moon, she is always giving credit to the Source of light which illuminates her by the very nature of her being, which is a gentle, quiet spirit. In the simplest of activities, sweeping the floor or preparing a meal, Faith does so in a peaceful, worshipful way maintaining her awareness of the Lord's presence. It is a subtle, behind-the-scenes servanthood, which might go unnoticed, were it not for the sublime attractiveness and power of its holiness.

I feel amazingly blessed to be married to Faith. It is simultaneously the most difficult and the most rewarding journey I have ever embarked on. As much as I played around before I got married, I can honestly and gratefully say that I'd rather be in dire straits with Faith within the covenant of our marriage than back there in a life of indulgent pleasures and worldly seductions—"free" by the world's definition.

The adage "You can't teach an old dog new tricks" takes on a slightly different meaning when it comes to a *bad* dog, the old me. The Lord brought me a woman who is so far out of my league in spiritual maturity, that it continually humbles the prideful part of me that considered myself to be a "ladies' man." The taking-for-granted attitude that became a strongly established pattern, knowing there was always another female just around the corner, is now subject to daily lessons in what it means to truly honor a woman—especially the one that

God has so clearly ordained just for me. I am getting sobered and schooled daily in moving from the exciting creativity of a Babylonian life (based on satisfying the senses) to a life of noble character in Christ.

So, if you still have any misunderstanding of why I'm Faith's *second favorite husband*, I will explain further. There is a reference in the Bible to people being promised as a pure bride to one husband—Christ (2 Corinthians 11:2). That's not just females promised to Christ as their husband. That's males, too. The correct relationship for someone who believes in Jesus Christ as their Lord and Savior is a covenant relationship—a marriage, as it were—in which the relationship is blessed by God's promises, beyond anything one does or doesn't do. It is a *gift* from God. Faith is married to the Lord and lives daily in her devotion to Him. As a Jew, one of God's chosen people, she is already a step ahead in her orientation toward Him, but through Christ she is *completed* in Him. What that means in simple terms is that her love for and sense of marriage to God is in her bones! It's very deep and inextricable.

I'm not sure about you, but for me as a man, being a bride doesn't come naturally. But, this is the amazing miracle of being married to Faith. In my daily witnessing of what a consecrated devotional life actually looks like, a life married to the Lord, I have been naturally led into what it is to be single pointed. I have learned to be faithful, both in my marriage to Faith and to the Lord, as well. Faith has been, and continues to be, an amazing servant of the Lord. In her presence I gain a full recognition of the brilliance of God's design for husband and wife to come together in a covenant marriage with each other, and with Him. Praise the Lord! What an incredible journey Home!

—*Justice*

Justice and Faith Collier